Property Management

Property Management

Douglas Scarrett BSc (Estate Management), FRICS

Principal Lecturer
Leicester Polytechnic, UK

LONDON   NEW YORK
E. & F. N. SPON

First published 1983 by
E. & F. N. Spon Ltd
11 New Fetter Lane, London EC4P 4EE
Published in the USA by
E. & F. N. Spon
733 Third Avenue, New York NY10017

Printed in Great Britain by J. W. Arrowsmith Ltd,
Bristol

ISBN 0 419 12380 6 (cased)
ISBN 0 419 12390 3 (paperback)

British Library Cataloguing in Publication Data

Scarrett, Douglas
    Property management.
    1. Real estate management—England
    I. Title
    333.33'0942   HD598

    ISBN 0—419—12380—6
    ISBN 0—419—12390—3 Pbk

Library of Congress Cataloging in Publication Data

Scarrett, Douglas, 1929—
    Property management.

    Includes index.
    1. Real estate management. I. Title.
HD1394.S27 1983 332.63'24'068 83—12515
ISBN 0—419—12380—6
ISBN 0—419—12390—3 (pbk.)

Contents

Preface

Ever since one man first granted authority to another to occupy his premises there has been a need for some sort of control to ensure that the occupier complied with his undertakings subject to which he had certain rights of enjoyment.

The activity of management has long been one of the strands of a surveyor's web, often regarded by the uninitiated as boring and demeaning. Properly carried out it is neither of these things but a highly complex function requiring considerable professional talent and knowledge: never has this been more true than today when vast sums are invested annually by insurance companies, pension funds and other institutions accountable to their members or shareholders.

This book attempts to suggest guidelines for good management practice of assistance to the busy property manager, whether dealing with a small number of modest properties or a large portfolio. It is hoped that this insight into management practice will be of interest to the student also.

The treatment of the material relevant to this vast subject is necessarily selective but it is hoped that the reader will gain at least an indication of the principles involved in good management. Most of the text is of universal application although the law is relevant only to England and Wales.

The errors that undoubtedly exist are hopefully few and minor. Much of what is written is the result of discussions with people in and beyond the profession, with clients and from experience over some years in practice and industry.

I am particularly grateful to a former colleague Mr Norman Withey for his assistance. Finally, my sincere thanks to my wife not only for her forbearance but for her encouragement and positive help in finding time to type the draft manuscript in an already busy life.

List of cases referred to in the text

List of statutes referred to in the text

Agricultural Holdings Act 1948
Agricultural Wages Act 1948
Agriculture Act 1967
Alkali Works Regulation Act 1906
Arbitration Act 1950
Arbitration Act 1979
Assured Tenancies (Approved Bodies) Orders

Clean Air Act 1956
Clean Air Act 1968
Cost of Leases Act 1958
Counter Inflation Act 1973
County Courts Act 1959

Defective Premises Act 1972
Development Land Tax Act 1976

Explosives Act 1875

Factories Act 1961
Finance Act 1965
Finance Act 1971
Fire Precautions Act 1971
Fireworks Act 1951
Food and Drugs Act 1955

General Rate Act 1967
Guard Dogs Act 1975

Health and Safety at Work Act 1974
Highways Act 1959
House of Commons Disqualification Act 1975
Housing Act 1957
Housing Act 1961

Housing Act 1974
Housing Act 1980
Housing Finance Act 1972

Land Charges Act 1972
Landlord and Tenant Act 1927
Landlord and Tenant Act 1954
Landlord and Tenant Act 1954 (Appropriate Multiplier) Regulations
      1981 (SI 1981/69)
Landlord and Tenant Act 1962
Law of Property Act 1922
Law of Property Act 1925
Law of Property Act 1969
Leasehold Reform Act 1967
Leasehold Reform Act 1979
Local Government & Planning Act 1980

Matrimonial Homes Act 1967

Noise Abatement Act 1960

Occupiers' Liability Act 1957
Offices, Shops and Railway Premises Act 1963

Petroleum (Consolidation) Act 1928
Plant and Machinery Order 1960
Plant and Machinery Order 1974
Protection from Eviction Act 1977
The Protected Tenancies (Exceptions)
The Protected Tenancies (Exceptions) Regulations 1974
      (SI No 1366)
Public Health Act 1936
Public Health Act 1961

Recorded Delivery Service Act 1962
Rent Act 1977
Rent (Agriculture) Act 1976
Rent Book (Forms of Notice) Regulations 1976 (SI 378)
Rentcharges Act 1977
Restricted Tenancies (Further Exceptions) Regulations 1976
      (SI No 905)

Shops Act 1950
The Solicitors Act 1957

Town and County Planning Acts 1947–71

CHAPTER 1

The role of property management

1.1 INTRODUCTION

Banks, insurance companies, building societies and many of the leading retailers own their operational premises where possible as a matter of policy. Manufacturers in the basic industries, especially where specialized plant is used with little or no conventional buildings, often have no option but to provide their premises, developers not being prepared to finance developments which often have no alternative use, suffer heavy wear and tear and are susceptible to technological change with a direct but uncertain effect on the economic life of the unit.

Many of the remaining retailers, office users and manufacturers take a conscious decision to lease their premises enabling available capital to be employed in the furtherance of their business activities.

The provision of premises for letting to these various users has become a major industry, almost entirely controlled by property companies, insurance companies, pension funds, local authorities and similar institutions.

These institutions have vast investments in property. For example, it is estimated that the insurance companies alone own investment property with a current value exceeding £14000m while local authority, public and private sector pension funds together own property with a value of some £7600m with a further £1400m held indirectly through property unit trusts. In 1982 further sums well in excess of £2000m were invested in property by insurance companies, pension funds and property unit trusts (Debenham, Tewson and Chinnocks *Money into Property 1970—1982*).

The majority of the investments by such groups is in commercial and industrial premises with a small proportion in agricultural land and virtually nothing in residential property.

A sizeable part of the housing stock is held by local authorities, housing associations, trusts and private landlords (the latter often controlling the poorest type of accommodation) and by public and private bodies for housing a part of their workforce or student population. There are companies which, by inheritance or design, own housing units. In most cases the company policy will be to dispose of any unit once vacant possession is obtained.

Certain public bodies may be required to make accommodation available for sale to the incumbent, subject to limited exceptions and at a considerable discount on the market value. Some organizations operate similar schemes on a voluntary basis.

To obtain the optimum return, these investments demand skilled day to day management, coupled with longer term planning and policy implementation. The manager will be concerned with such matters as contractual relationships and the need for searching interpretation of leases; the effect of statutory intervention and revenue and capital tax provisions; the achievement of streamlined and efficient management; the continuing upgrading of a portfolio to secure a balanced mix, safe growth and the reduction of risk. Modern property management requires the contributions of several specialisms but the professional surveyor not only occupies a dominant role but also in many cases leads the team. He may be employed in public service or in private practice: he may be in the full time salaried employ of an institution or he may act as an agent of his several principals on a fee or commission basis. In-house managers often supplement their skills and abilities by the employment of private practitioners for special tasks or for certain limited management functions.

1.2 DEFINITION

Management may be defined simply as the implementation of policy decisions and the accomplishment of objectives.

There is no shortage of published advice on the many aspects of management though most is concerned with the production process and the efficient control of a labour force. While the principles of management apply to a wide variety of situations, their application is of necessity somewhat different where property is managed. There is no end-product in the accepted sense of something manufactured and management is undertaken in many cases by an agent for a principal rather than by an employee for his employer.

Furthermore, important aspects of property management are not predictable or repetitive and the manager's instructions should provide for a degree of flexibility. So, although the elements of organization, policy implementation and decision making are all present, a specific attempt at a definition of property management is necessary:

Property management seeks to control property interests having regard to the short and long term objectives of the estate owner and particularly to the purpose for which the interest is held: to negotiate lettings and to initiate and negotiate rent reviews and lease renewals, to oversee physical maintenance and enforcement of lease covenants, to be mindful of the necessity of upgrading and merging interests where possible, to recognize opportunities for the development of potential and to fulfil the owner's legal and social duties to the community.

The procedure by which these objectives are achieved will vary according to the method of property management followed and the way in which policy is formulated and decisions are made. Policy will be dictated by numerous considerations directed towards achieving the owner's objectives: while the principles of good property management practice will normally be followed, there may be occasions when good practice will be overridden by the need to achieve a particular objective of the estate owner.

Exploration of the various parts of this definition will be deferred until later chapters but it is pertinent to remark here that proposals for the future use of a property often raise sensitive public issues when it becomes desirable to consider the effect of the proposal on adjoining owners or properties or on the community. These considerations go beyond the concern of planning control or the private legal rights of others to suggest that a responsible reaction to serious and informed public opinion may well be more productive in the long run than unnecessary confrontation. Of course, there will be cases where property management considerations dictate that an unpopular course of action is pursued vigorously even in the face of public opposition.

1.3   OBJECTIVES OF PROPERTY MANAGEMENT

The objectives of property management will normally be the maximization of income and capital but not necessarily so: the motive of the owner in acquiring the interest will be relevant.

The investor who seeks to use his capital to provide a good low risk return may well be indifferent as to the type of investment chosen: where he invests in real estate he will no doubt expect to obtain as high a rent as is compatible with safety and ease of management which includes finding a financially sound tenant and engaging him in a satisfactory form of lease enabling the landlord, among other things, to maintain the purchasing power of his income by provision for regular and frequent reviews of rent levels.

A very few owners may be interested in providing a service by offering accommodation free or at a price below its current value, as where almshouses were provided in the past by charities. But most of the present custodians of residential estates created by the early social reformers have long since embraced the system of fair rents in an attempt to make them self supporting: some have even been broken up under financial pressures. The modern collective conscience, as genuinely represented by many housing associations, draws support and subsidy from central funds in the form of grants to replace any shortfall of income incurred.

Short and long term objectives need to be considered separately.

1.3.1   Short term objectives

The short term objectives are often the obvious ones: the

collection of rents, prevention of arrears, increase of rent roll, enforcement of lease provisions in relation to landlord's and tenant's covenants — especially repairing covenants — and adequate insurance cover. But, in addition, care must be taken in day to day management that longer term objectives are not prejudiced unwittingly.

1.3.2 Longer term objectives

The longer term objectives may be simply the perpetuation of the short term ones as will be the case with a prime investment holding. However, the majority of investments will offer scope for long term improvement to the benefit of the capital and or rental values of the property. Examples include the merger of interests (e.g. the enlargement of a leasehold interest by purchase of the freehold reversion), the extinguishment of restrictive covenants or the rights of others over the property, the acquisition of adjoining property especially where a redevelopment site is being assembled, the rationalization of leases particularly so as to be co-terminous and a reduction in detailed management by renegotiation where the opportunity presents itself on reletting or where the tenant wishes to renegotiate his lease for one reason or another. Where possible, the quality of tenant will be improved and multiple lettings reduced to single occupations.

Many external factors are beyond the control of the owner: an outdated warehouse on several floors or shop premises in a part of the town centre no longer fashionable with the major traders are likely to defy even the most determined and expensive efforts at upgrading, although there may be opportunities for change of use or redevelopment of the site. The intention of detailed management may be to improve the property for retention in the portfolio or to present it as free of problems as is possible for sale to an investor with different objectives, reinvesting the proceeds in a more appropriate way.

The property manager will bear in mind that capital value may be improved substantially where a full repairing and insuring lease with frequent rent reviews can be negotiated with a substantial tenant.

1.4 THE ESTATE OWNER

It was remarked earlier that the owner of a substantial property is much more likely to be an institution or a corporation than an individual.

The considerations of management will be determined to a large extent by the declared purpose of the organization and the need to satisfy various interested parties — shareholders, policy holders, pension recipients, the Registrar of Friendly Societies and the Charity Commissioners among others — that the investment is being managed in an appropriate way. These requirements leave little room for the benevolent landlord. Good management and the identification and exploitation of potential are essential to the well-being of a commercially orientated company.

Duties may arise from obligations accepted in a lease to a tenant imposed by a head-lease or conveyance or necessary to comply with statutory provisions.

Where the duty is substantial and certain to arise at some time in the future, the owner should consider building up a reserve or providing a sinking fund to meet the estimated cost. Where the contingent liability is based on the existence of a legal requirement, as for example a restrictive covenant entered into many years ago, probably by a predecessor in title, it may be possible to insure against the unlikely event of a third party claiming the benefit of and enforcing the covenant.

Should the opportunity arise to remove a liability (by purchase, merger, negotiation or exchange) it should receive serious consideration even though no immediate benefit is conferred.

1.5 MANAGEMENT IN PRACTICE

In numerous firms, the function of property management has been carried on for many years. Some firms have undertaken the work without any enthusiasm, because their clients expect it of them and because it maintains contact with the client and other work tends to follow. Others regard the unspectacular but regular fee income as a useful foundation, perhaps offering more freedom in other spheres of the practice. Still others undertake management for its own sake and achieve considerable success through their positive approach.

Whichever route is followed, the property manager occupies a crucial role in the landlord—tenant relationship. He is most likely to act for the landlord but his services may sometimes be of assistance to the tenant also and not only in the area of rent reviews and lease renewals.

It is probably true that the opportunity to manage important property portfolios is less likely to present itself to the small provincial firm, than to the London or large regional practice. But there is no reason why the smaller firm should be at any disadvantage in providing an efficient management service in its own locality. It is, of course, necessary for the department to be properly founded, organized and staffed. Property management must provide the surest route for a discerning client to form a view as to the efficiency and ability of a particular firm.

With these remarks in mind, the following check list is suggested:

What is the purpose of the department?
  Is the department seen as an essential part of an overall property service to clients or is it being provided reluctantly and without enthusiasm? Is it the intention to do what is necessary to collect rents and deal with problems as they arise or to provide positive and dynamic management designed to exploit the potential of the property managed?

What limitations will be placed on operations?
  Many firms will not wish to manage the older types of residential property while few, unless specially set up, will be able to undertake the management of furnished premises.

What development plans are there?
  The department may expand by obtaining further management work or by offering additional services (e.g. regular revaluations, architectural and building supervisory services, taxation negotiations) or by a combination of both.

Where should the offices be situated?
  It may not be necessary to occupy the same building as is used by the remainder of the firm especially if cheaper and more efficient offices may be obtained nearby.

Who is to take charge?

As much as in any other department, leadership should be
provided by a partner or an experienced and senior member
of the professional staff. His involvement should be sub-
stantive but he should avoid becoming so much involved
with detail as to be unable to take a detached and objective
view of the whole department.

What staff is required?

Property management is a very time consuming operation.
While much of the repetitive work may now be allocated
to computers, much work remains which, by its very
nature, cannot be programmed or even forecast yet must
receive prompt and efficient attention when it arises. This
suggests not only adequate staffing levels to cope with
unexpected and peak demands but a degree of inter-
changeability which may be difficult to achieve with any
level of expertise at least in the smaller practice. Professional,
technical, administrative and secretarial assistance will be
essential to any property management department although
in the smaller office some grouping of skills may take place.

What provision is to be made for staff training?

Even experienced staff need to keep up to date, which
may be achieved by means of short courses, refresher
courses, reading or transfer within the firm. The staff
should be encouraged to recognize their contribution to
the overall process of management.

What back-up services are needed?

The property manager should maintain a good resource
unit of relevant books, magazines, articles and literature
on builders' materials and practices and especially of legal
text-books and reports of law cases. A supply of statutory
and non-statutory forms and notices should also be held.
Such a library must be up to date to be of any value and is
likely to work effectively only if a particular person has
the responsibility for it.

What level of charges is to be imposed?

Is the operation of the department to be subsidized by
other departments of the firm or is it required to be self
financing? Is the management charge to be on a per-

centage basis of the rent, or is an appropriate management fee to be negotiated?

How is contact with clients to be maintained?

The firm should consider whether contact with at least the larger clients should not be maintained by formal meetings at regular intervals. It would be possible to report on the general performance of each investment and to discuss the future of individual investments and the strategy for the holding and to obtain instructions.

1.6 THE FUTURE

The demand for skilled, capable and imaginative managers is unlikely to diminish. Even allowing for real differences between the property market and the market in stocks and shares, there is a long way to go before the sophistication of the investment analyst is matched in the property field. Some advances in techniques and interpretation will be demanded by owners who may be about to witness a slowing down of rental growth with consequent effects on capital value.

Present economic conditions and the state of business confidence are not conducive to schemes of comprehensive redevelopment and the current level of building costs now more often renders many propositions unviable. The alleged relationship between inflation and growth is no longer pursued as vigorously as once it was and it is no longer expected that rents will increase almost automatically in line with or ahead of the rate of inflation. Those properties purchased at an optimistically low initial yield will require all the expertise and ingenuity of their managers to avoid the worst embarrassments of any failure to achieve the growth implied by the price paid.

The onset of a tenant's market is not likely to witness wholesale movements by tenants: those properties satisfactory to the purpose of the tenant will continue to be occupied although he may be unable and or unwilling to agree a higher level of rent on review or renewal unless the proposal is supported by substantial market evidence.

The well-being of the property market is inextricably

linked to the commercial and manufacturing bases of the country. Writing in March 1981 in the 1980 Annual Report of Imperial Chemical Industries Ltd the chairman, Sir Maurice Hodgson, observed:

> In responding to the events of 1980 we have to distinguish between the cyclical effects of recession and the longer term structural changes which are taking place in our business environment.

While these sober remarks may have been intended primarily to reflect the situation in the chemical industry it is at least possible that they may prove prophetic for a much wider business community with implications for institutions, investors and managers.

The introduction of modern office aids — especially electronic equipment, the use of which is explored in the final chapter — will present the manager with a new freedom and an opportunity to address himself to the philosophies of management so essential to achieve the most advantageous results.

FURTHER READING

Allsopp, J. M. (1979) *Management in the Professions*, Business Books, London.

Ratcliffe, J. (1978) *An Introduction to Urban Land Administration*, Estate Gazette, London.

Stapleton, T. (1981) *Estate Management Practice*, Estates Gazette, London.

Thorncroft, M. (1965) *Principles of Estate Management*, Estates Gazette, London.

CHAPTER 2

Records

2.1 INTRODUCTION

Accurate, comprehensive and up-to-date records are a prerequisite of efficient property management. Failure to
initiate and maintain adequate records could well result in
an important date being overlooked or a necessary item of
information not being available when required: the consequence of any such failure could be far reaching: it could
lead to a loss of trust or confidence by the client, such
necessary elements in the relationship, or in more serious
cases to a claim against the manager or firm based on negligence.

There are interesting aspects to the subject of records. A
firm may have been responsible for the management of a
property since it was built or it may have taken over the
management from another agent or from the owner. The
record system in use may have been designed when the firm
was responsible for the management of a very modest collection of properties: what was suitable then is unlikely to be
wholly appropriate to the management of a large portfolio
of property, spread over a region or even throughout the
country, particularly having regard to the incidence of
taxation and in particular capital taxation and to the various
forms of statutory intervention. Furthermore, an owner may
delegate the whole of the management of his properties to his
agent or the agent may play only a limited role. While uni-
formity is desirable, different owners may identify a different
range of requirements: finally it must be remembered that
each property is unique.

It is worth observing that electronically-based technology
is ideally placed to make a significant contribution to proper

management without disturbing any of its basic tenets. Indeed, this aspect is so important that it is explored in more detail in a later chapter. With these remarks in mind, the remainder of this chapter will be devoted to a study of the principal records necessary in an efficient practice and to the considerations necessary in the design of such records.

2.2   PURPOSES OF RECORDS

In essence, office records should achieve a detailed account of the property and of the instructions of the owner together with adequate information about the occupier. The most immediately important information will be that concerning the current position but there are many occasions when it is necessary to produce historical information concerning, for example, acquisition, works of improvement or details of an earlier tenancy, while without a knowledge of future events concerning the property it will not be possible to give proper consideration to advice on future strategy. We are concerned not only with past present and future but also with both physical and legal aspects of ownership. Some of this information will be available in original documents: some may be obtained by an examination of the building and some from an inspection of a correspondence file or from incidents within the knowledge of one of the members of staff. The first three means of retrieval are time consuming and inefficient where the information is capable of classification, the last is dangerous and should be avoided even if only by making a contemporary note and placing it in the file.

To sum up, then, the records required — excluding, for the time being, the mechanisms to demand collect and account for rent and to sanction the payment of expenses — will be divided between physical and legal aspects of the property, some of which will have lasting utility while others will be of only fleeting significance.

2.3   DESIGNING A RECORD SYSTEM

It is unlikely that an 'off-the-peg' system will be found that will operate satisfactorily in every respect in the particular circumstances of the management organization and its responsibilities.

Nevertheless, certain basic principles may be laid down. The prerequisite of any system of records is to understand why it is necessary. Where, as in property management, the operation has a technical background it is desirable that any system is designed if not in consultation with the user then at least with an understanding of his needs. Some discipline and clear thinking is needed to avoid incorporating parts of existing systems simply because that information has always been available. Each of the following questions needs to be posed and answered and the answers borne in mind throughout the period of design:

(a) What is required of the system?
(b) What information is necessary to meet these requirements?
(c) How best can the information be extracted, assembled and presented?
(d) Will the system operate quickly and efficiently?

with the implication that no extraneous information will be recorded.

A small but important point is that all forms, record cards, sheets and other stationery should be produced to conform to international metric sizes, the more common of which are:

Reference	Size		Suggested use
	(mm)	*(in.)*	
A1	594 x 841	23.39 x 33.11	Plans and
A2	420 x 594	16.54 x 23.39	drawings
A3	297 x 420	11.69 x 16.54	Leases
A4	210 x 297	8.27 x 11.69	Forms
A5	148 x 210	5.83 x 8.27	Forms
A6	105 x 148	4.13 x 5.83	Record cards
A7	74 x 105	2.91 x 4.13	Record cards

The responsibilities of various levels of staff should be established at an early stage and in a large organization there are likely to be three tiers of operation:

Type of work	Performed by
Routine, repetitive	Clerical staff
Interpretative	Technical staff
Decision making, advisory	Professional staff

While not always possible, it is good practice for work to be allocated by a senior member of staff: not only is he able to control individual work loads but also he has early warning of any potentially difficult or significant situations. Decisions need to be made on the layout and typeface of forms and as to whether one copy of a form is to be circulated in sequence to each section of the organization or whether each section will receive and retain its own copy. Colour coding of forms or cards in an index system can be used with advantage, increasing the speed of identification or information and reducing the possibility of mis-filing.

The following proposals for an efficient record system are intended to be adapted to the particular needs of the organization using the system: those needs are likely to be determined by the size and complexity of the units being managed, the extent of the management responsibility, the degree of sophistication sought and the cost of the operation in relation to the fees charged.

2.4   FILE REFERENCES

A number of files or sections of files are suggested in respect of each unit of management: for example, a large office block let to say twelve separate tenants would have a file for each of those tenants in addition to one or more owner's files. One way of dealing with a large number of properties is to allocate a reference number to each property with a further division for each tenancy. For example, a lock-up shop separately let from the offices about it would have the main (owner's) reference say 90 while any divisions of that file thought necessary (insurance, service charges) would be numbered 90A, 90B and so on.

The tenants' files would become

Shop   90/1
Offices 90/2

All letters, orders, statements, demands and other items relating to the property would bear the appropriate reference number.

As a further aid to efficiency, the owners' and tenants' files could be colour coded.

2.4.1 Survey file

A physical survey should be made of the buildings and site sufficient to enable a site plan and floor plans to be prepared. Where plans are available they should be checked and any inaccuracies or alterations noted. Details of construction, finishes, plant and machinery should be noted and the existence of wayleaves, easements, rights of light and similar rights whether these exist for the benefit of the subject property or adjoining property. Apparent boundaries should be checked against any information available in the title deeds, together with the ownership and responsibility for the maintenance of those boundaries. The plans could usefully be supported by photographs, one of which should show adjoining buildings also.

2.4.2 Title file

Copies of the main title documents would enable the manager to see the precise nature of a restrictive covenant, or boundary maintenance responsibility, and enable him to act swiftly and decisively where demanded by the circumstances. Any legal problems beyond his ability or brief would be referred to the client or to his solicitor: possession of title documents would ensure that his report was apposite.

2.4.3 Insurance file

Whether or not the owner is responsible for insuring the premises, he will need to be satisfied by the manager that the cover both for risks and for reinstatement cost is adequate. For this purpose a detailed insurance valuation should be prepared — in conjunction with a quantity surveyor if necessary. The figure arrived at will then form the basis of an annual review, the detailed build-up being re-examined every three or five years.

Except in the case of large buildings, this file could form part of the survey file.

2.4.4 The terrier

A loose-leaf book or card index system giving brief up-to-date details of each property, owner, tenants, rents, repairing and other responsibilities of the parties, insurance cover, rent reviews, lease expirations and similar information. The terrier is intended to give no more than a broad picture, precise details being settled by reference to one or other of the main files.

One of the weaknesses of any system and particularly of a record such as a terrier is that often it is not kept up to date in which case its use may be positively dangerous.

An example of a terrier sheet is given in Fig. 2.1.

2.4.5 Perpetual diary

Whenever a lease is entered into there are certain future events about which the property manager will need to be alerted to enable him to take any action necessary. For example, he will need to be reminded that the lease is coming to an end to enable him to negotiate a new lease with the occupier or find a new tenant: he will wish to check that external painting which the tenant has undertaken to renew at intervals has in fact been carried out: and he will need to set in motion the appropriate machinery, as laid down in the lease, for any agreed rent reviews. This last example is particularly important where a missed review can sour relations with a client and may prove costly to the manager or his professional indemnity company. For this reason, this part of the perpetual diary is often maintained separately by one of the professional staff.

One method of noting rent reviews or lease expiries which is capable of coping with all but the largest managements is to list each property by a single line entry on an index card filed under the name of the month in which the event occurs:

Reference	Address	Tenant	Term/Review	Expires
90/1	7 Cheap St	J. Marks	7 years from 2/78	February 1985
73/9	1 Light Rd	A. Johns	5 years from 2/76	February 1981
12/6	Suite 3, Hope House	D. Cole	7 years from 2/79	February 1986

ADDRESS		
O.S. Reference	Post code	
Owner's name		
Address		
Telephone No:		

Brief description: Number of floors   Gross internal area

Construction

Accommodation

Use class

Details of current letting:

Length of lease   Rent reviews

Term from   to

Initial rent £   First review £   Second review £

Let to

address (if different)

Tel number   Name of contact

Responsibility for

	Landlord	Tenant
Main walls and roof		
External repairs		
Internal repairs		
Decoration –external		
–internal		
Maintenance of service installations		
Common services		
Insurance		

Special notes:

Fig. 2.1 Terrier sheet

The cards would then be inspected yearly in the appropriate month. In this example, the first entry would require a file to be raised in February 1984 and the appropriate action commenced. The second listed property should have been dealt with following a perusal of the card in February 1980 and transferred to another card on completion of negotiations. No action is necessary on the third entry until February 1985. (The operation of the system should take account of the few situations where a warning period of one year is insufficient.)

There is a need for a 'follow-up' system to ensure that the owner's instructions are obtained and negotiations opened with the tenant or a new tenant sought. On completion of negotiations, the entry would be deleted and an appropriate new entry recorded.

Each month would form a separate section of the index.

The above files may be regarded as the permanent records of the property, being in use throughout the period of management. There follows a description of files which will tend to last for the currency of the tenancy.

2.4.6   Lease file

While it is desirable to have copies of the title documents, it is essential to have copies of the current lease of each unit managed. The lease provisions will be summarized in the terrier and significant dates recorded in the perpetual calendar, but it will often prove necessary to consult the precise wording of the document.

2.4.7   Management, services and repair files

There may be some advantage in particular circumstances in having separate files but in general one file should be sufficient to cover general management, service provision and repair items. Where the tenant is responsible for maintenance at specified intervals, inspection dates will be recorded in the perpetual diary.

2.5   STATISTICAL USES

In completing returns, reporting to owners or preparing advice or evidence (e.g. in rent review arbitrations) it is important that information is available in the form required for the particular purpose. The records should be classified in such a way that it is possible, for example, to say what proportion of a client's holding or of the total management is in office use in units of up to 5000 square feet and how many of the leases of such holdings are due to expire each year for the next five years. Fortunately the collation and presentation of such information now requires no more than a simple computer program.

2.6   RETENTION OF RECORDS

It is established office procedure to specify retention periods for each type of record having regard to usefulness and legal obligations on the one hand and the pressure of space on the other. Very few property management files can be disposed of: matters concerning improvements to the premises or a question of taxation may be pertinent long after a particular letting has terminated or the premises have been sold. The problem becomes one of efficient storage. The file may be 'weeded' but it is not always possible to know which papers to remove and which to retain: there are dangers in an incomplete file. An alternative is to record the whole of the file on microfilm. Not only are copies of all the papers available for viewing, but the storage space required is only a fraction of the space occupied by the original file.

FURTHER READING

Mills, G. and Standingford, O. (1978) *Office Organization and Method*, Pitman Publishing, London.
Tavernier, G. (1972) *Basic Office Systems and Records*, Gower Press, Farnborough.

CHAPTER 3

Accounting procedure

3.1 INTRODUCTION

The basic accounting procedure will be modified according to the particular circumstances of management. An in-house accounting system for a portfolio owned by one company will be a good deal more simple and straightforward than the system required where several hundred clients own a wide variety of properties.

The requirements of any system are that it should record transactions, provide a statement of receipts and payments, and transfer funds at agreed intervals. This chapter will explore those requirements and propose a system suitable for the most common style of management, i.e. where properties are managed for a number of clients.

3.2 OBJECTIVES

The objectives of any such system may now be considered in more detail.

3.2.1 Accuracy

Accuracy is a prerequisite of any system. While a simple system avoids various possibilities of error, the procedure should be sufficiently sophisticated to be able to digest and process a variety of receipts and outgoings.

3.2.2 Immediacy

The client's account may be called upon at any time to make quite substantial payments to or on behalf of the owner. It is essential that the decision to release a sum of money is based on the latest financial position of the accounts. The two senior professional bodies have introduced Members' Accounts Regulations. In the preface to the Regulations made by the General Council of the Royal Institution of Chartered Surveyors, it is explained that

> 'The principal object of the Members' Accounts Regulations is to ensure the maintenance of an adequate book-keeping and recording system in order that Members may be assisted in the management of their clients' affairs and of their practices.'

Regulation 4 limits the monies to be paid into a client account thus:

(a) such money belonging to the Member as may be the minimum required by the bank for the purpose of opening or maintaining that account;
(b) money to replace any sum which for any reason may have been drawn from the account in contravention of these Regulations.

To which note (ii) to Regulation 1 and notes (iii) and (v) to Regulation 6 are particularly relevant:

Regulation 1

(ii)   A 'float' put in by a Member to keep his client account in balance is not clients' money, and, in any case, may only be done within the provisions of Regulation 4(a). It may be thought, on the face of it, that Regulation 4(a) might give the necessary authority for a Member to 'top up' his client account, but this is not so; Regulation 4(a) is restricted to the nominal sum (if any) required to open the client account at a bank.

Regulation 6

(iii)   It should be noted that drawing money on behalf of a client from a client account when such drawing exceeds the total of the money held on behalf of that client is not permissible. In order to comply with this Regulation, in a situation where there are insufficient funds in an individual client's ledger to meet a particular payment, the procedures must be:

(a) either draw one cheque on the client account to the extent of the funds held on behalf of that particular client, and another cheque on the firm's accounts for the balance; or

(b) transfer sufficient firm's money to the client's ledger (with the appropriate transfer of funds to the client account), and then draw a cheque on the client account for the total sum required.

The underlying reason for this requirement lies in the rules which apply in the case of a bankruptcy, since it is essential that clients' money can be identified as such.

(v)   It will be appreciated that a Member should use caution in drawing against a cheque before it has been cleared as in the event of it being dishonoured a shortage of clients' funds would arise. The Member can avoid a breach of the Regulations by instructing his bank, if practicable, to charge all unpaid credits to his office or personal bank account.

3.2.3   Promptness

One of the attractions of investment in property is the regular nature of the income. The property manager should uphold the agreed accounting dates and ensure that the client is notified when circumstances outside his control make it likely that the statement will not be posted on time. The organization should be flexible enough to ensure that accounting tasks do not fall behind particularly at the work peaks which are an inevitable feature of most management accounting. Some preparation of statements may be done in advance or staff may be given different or additional responsibilities at these times. The introduction of computers with appropriate accounting programs will enable these problems of manual accounting to be overcome.

3.2.4   Proof against fraud

Balancing checks will normally show up mistakes or omissions in bookkeeping but it is necessary to take precautions against the possibility of deliberate fraud. A precise system, properly operated, is the best defence. Authorization of payments should be strictly limited and consideration given to the requirement of two signatures on cheques for more than a stipulated amount. Care should be taken not to create an opportunity for a member of staff to be wholly in control of a particular operation: it is not popular but nonetheless useful to change the tasks undertaken by members of staff at regular intervals. In addition to taking all possible precautions, an adequate fidelity policy should be arranged and reviewed at frequent intervals.

3.3 THE ACCOUNTING RECORDS

The accounting system now proposed suggests the broad arrangement of a manual scheme suitable for a medium to

Address	
Owner	
Tel No.	Solicitor:
Use class	
Gross internal floor area	Floor plan ref:
Insurance cover Risks All/Fire	Amount 19.... £
	19.... £
	19.... £
Rent £ p.a.	
Next review due	
Landlord's responsibility for repairs	
Authority for expenditure up to £	
Statements monthly/quarterly – dates	
Cheque to owner/bank	
Let to	

Fig. 3.1 Master record card

large size management practice. Individual needs and preferences will determine sheet sizes, loose-leaf or bound
format, colour coding and other detail.

3.3.1   Master record card

Figure 3.1 shows the master record card which carries all
permanent information relating to the owner including the
extent of delegated authority for incurring expenditure and
the rate of commission or other method of charging agreed
with the owner. The 'master' may be regarded as the financial
terrier: it is used as the source of information in relation to
the preparation of periodic financial statements to the owner.

3.3.2   Tenant record card

Adjacent to each master record card is a set of tenant record
cards, one for each separate lease. The information contained
on the card should be sufficient to enable a rent demand to

Address
Tenant Address Tel No. Contact
Rent £ Next review Repairing liabilities
Business of tenant Use of premises
Additional information

Fig. 3.2 Tenant record card

be prepared with information on charges for other items such as insurance premiums and services together with any increased rent recoverable under the lease at some future date (see Fig. 3.2).

3.3.3 Rent demand

While not part of the primary accounting system, the rent demand is referred to here because it follows from the tenant record card. In a manual system, the most economical method is to prepare the demand and three copies. The original (Fig. 3.3) is addressed to the tenant and sets out the address

Fig. 3.3 Rent demand (Demand on three copies (Figs 3.4, 3.5 and 3.6) typed at same time on NCR paper)

of the leased premises, the amount of rent and other charges and the due date. Further copies are prepared at the same time, the preprinted part of each carrying a different message. The second copy reminds the tenant that he is in arrear with payment (Fig. 3.4) the third gives information to the client's solicitor in the event of the rent remaining unpaid after a period of say 21 days (Fig. 3.5) while the final copy (Fig. 3.6) records receipt of the amount due and enables the proper details to be posted in the rent ledger.

It is likely that some tenants will wish to make payment by direct debit and other tenants should be encouraged to pay in this way. The tenant may either specify an amount in

A B and Son
Managing Agents

Date:

Dear Sir(s)

One [month's/quarter's] rent was due on [date] in respect of your occupation of

[address]

We regret to note that the amount of £ has not yet been received. Please forward by return to avoid the necessity of further action

Yours faithfully

A B and Son

To

[Tenant]

Fig. 3.4 Rent demand copy (reminder)

A B and Son
Managing Agents

Date:

Dear Sir(s)

One [month's/quarter's] rent due on [date]
remains unpaid in respect of

[address]

The arrears amount to £
and we shall be pleased if you will take action on behalf
of the owners

Yours faithfully
A B and Son

Tenant

To
X Y and Son
Solicitors

Owner:

Fig. 3.5 Rent demand copy (instructions to solicitor on default by tenant)

his instructions to his bank or give authority for an unspecified amount to be paid to the property manager or his banker at appropriate intervals. The latter arrangement enables variable payments to be collected. Where payments are made by direct debit, it will be necessary to obtain confirmation that the payment has been received.

3.3.4 Day book

Individual day books may be maintained for each type of receipt and outgoing or a multi-column book may be used

```
A B and Son
Managing Agents


                                      Date:

Dear Sir(s)
        One ⌈month's/quarter's⌉ rent due ⌈date⌉
is acknowledged in respect of
⌈address⌉



        Total payment              £



                        Yours faithfully
                            A B and Son

To
⌈Tenant⌉
```

Fig. 3.6 Rent demand copy (used as receipt)

to record all transactions as they occur, irrespective of the
owner or tenant concerned (Fig. 3.7).

3.3.5   Ledger
Each ledger account refers to the transactions of one owner
only and enables a statement to be prepared when due
(Fig. 3.8).

3.3.6   Statement
Each owner will expect to receive a statement and a cheque

Date	Description	Fo	Rent	Rates	Ins'ce	Repairs	Services	Sundries

Fig. 3.7 Day book

for the amount due on the dates agreed. A balance needs to be struck between the amount of detail included in the statement and the information which a client may properly expect and which he may need for tax returns, capital transfer tax calculations and so forth. Inadequate information at this stage may lead to additional work for the manager at a later date when it is often more time consuming to provide information required by the client.

A form of statement is illustrated in Fig. 3.9.

The way in which the financial records relate to one another is shown in diagrammatic form in Fig. 3.10.

3.3.7 Anticipated expenditure

It is important that any system devised is capable of alerting the person preparing the statement to the likelihood of accounts for payment being received in the near future.

Client:

Date	Receipts		Date	Payments	

Fig. 3.8 Ledger

		A B and Co Statement of Account		
Client:			Reference:	

Date	Description	Payments	Receipts
	Balance due	£	
	Cheque for balance enclosed/paid to the credit of your account		

Fig. 3.9 Statement

Regular payment for items such as insurance may be identified from the master record card but the order form for a non-recurring item should be duplicated and a copy attached to the master record card. In this way, consideration may be given to the need for a retention to meet the anticipated liability when accounting to the client.

3.3.8   Commission and VAT accounts

When statements are being prepared, the amount charged as commission for management of the property is calculated and deducted as an expense, being transferred to the commission account and at intervals to the income account of the practice.

Similarly, VAT is payable on most commission accounts and on other outputs, e.g. provision of services in a shopping development. The amounts should be recorded separately and forwarded to Customs and Excise at three-monthly periods.

Chapter 11 contains further information on this tax.

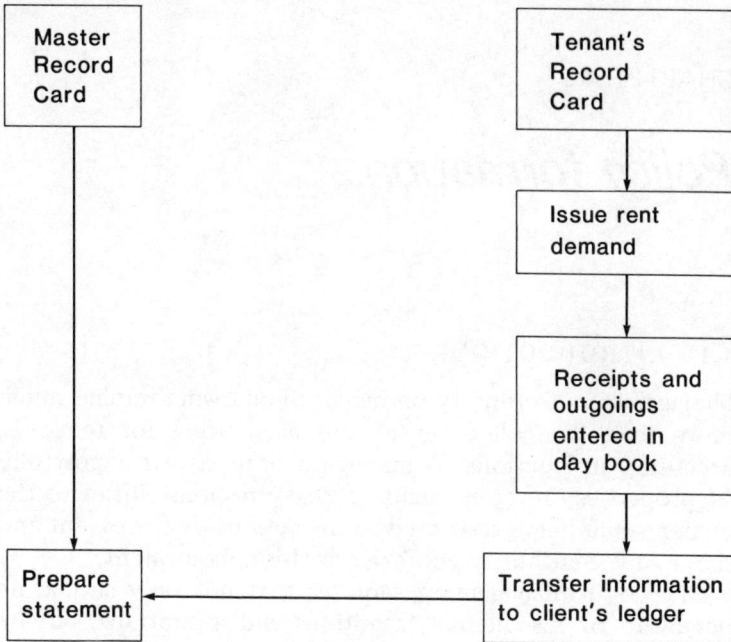

Fig. 3.10 Relationship of financial records

3.4 MISCELLANEOUS MATTERS

It is an important part of the manager's function to keep each client informed of events affecting his property and he will often find it useful to write a letter with the statement explaining any items which may not be clear drawing attention to any problems experienced or anticipated.

Reporting on broader issues is one of the subjects of the next chapter.

FURTHER READING

Edey, H. C. (1978) *Introduction to Accounting*, Hutchinson, London.
Wood, F. (1979) *Business Accounting*, volume 1, Longman Group, London.
Wood, F. (1980) *Business Accounting*, volume 2, Longman Group, London.

CHAPTER 4

Policy formation

4.1 INTRODUCTION

Management of property on behalf of an owner implies much more than the collection of and accounting for rents. In accepting instructions to manage a property or a portfolio of properties, an agent assumes heavy responsibilities to the owner while being restricted in his actions by the extent and scope of the authority conferred by his appointment.

Successful management requires that not only should he be aware of his client's intentions and aspirations, but he should also be prepared to contribute to the process of change where demanded by external events or dictated by the developing needs and philosophy of the owner. Such requirements imply frequent and regular contact, the form of which will be determined by agreement between the parties. Comprehensive management advice often requires the integration of various skills and disciplines and may involve the client's solicitor, accountant and others in addition to the property manager. These combined services are often indispensable but necessarily costly, one of a number of reasons for the eclipse of the private owner of a few modest properties in favour of the specialist property investment group.

4.2 LETTER OF APPOINTMENT

The basis of a satisfactory stewardship is a formal letter of appointment. It is in the interests of both parties for the terms of the appointment to be precise and unambiguous and a written appointment is much to be preferred. Aspects covered by the appointment should include the following.

4.2.1 Terms

The basis of the charge for collecting rents and other payment and for undertaking the other functions of management is usually a percentage of the amount collected. There are circumstances where it would be more equitable for a fixed charge to be agreed, related to the amount, intricacy or responsibility of work required or anticipated. A method gaining in popularity in some professions is 'time charging', where time spent is recorded in a diary and charged out at the rate appropriate to the position of the person undertaking the work. At present, adjustments tend to take the form of an alteration of the commission level which is somewhat arbitrary. Commission on insurance policies effected through the manager's agency is usually retained by him and by agreement with the client and in return for which he undertakes to advise on the level and extent of insurance cover. The matter of commission should be covered by express arrangements so as to avoid the possibility of any misunderstanding.

4.2.2 Authority

The extent of the agent's authority should be defined, particularly where it exceeds the usual duties of collection of rent and routine day to day management. Any extension is likely to be by way of specific limitation: for example, when authorizing the agent to order repair work without prior consultation, the owner will stipulate a maximum cost beyond which his instructions must first be sought. Payments to third parties and negotiations with tenants are other areas where the client will wish to limit the authority of his agent.

4.2.3 Procedure

In the general run of management it is sometimes necessary to employ the professional services of another: for example, a solicitor would need to be engaged where court action was to be initiated for arrears of rent. It is often necessary for such matters to be undertaken with the minimum of delay and the adoption of an agreed procedure will be in the client's interest, particularly where he may not be readily available for consultation for long periods.

4.2.4   Statements

In proposing a time-table for submission of statements the agent should arrange to account on a regular basis and within a few days of receipt of the rent payment. For most commercial property, a quarterly statement is likely to be satisfactory. Where any account for payment is due or anticipated at the statement date, the agent should arrange to retain a sum sufficient to enable him to discharge the account when received. There should also be firm arrangements with the client to avoid any deficit in the account arising from payment of an authorized outgoing.

4.3   CURRENT EVENTS

Any matters of importance affecting the property will be notified to the owner when they occur especially when a decision is required from him but many routine items may be deferred and included in a report enclosed with the statement. Each occasion should be seen as an opportunity to keep the owner in touch with matters of interest and possibly of some significance. The fact that, for example, a tenant's business is outgrowing his premises, that difficulty is being experienced in finding a firm able to repair an obsolete heating system, that construction of a proposed new road is about to be commenced or an indication of the level of rent achieved for similar nearby premises are all potentially useful items of information.

The manager will also keep the owner informed on new lettings, rent reviews and expiry of leases and take his instructions having offered advice.

4.4   LONG TERM PLANNING

On receipt of instructions to undertake management, the manager will wish to acquaint himself with the properties. He will find it useful to prepare a report for his client in which he deals not only with the present condition of each property, the need for repair or improvement and breaches of covenant but also with such matters as the economic amalgamation of tenancies and units, improvement of the type of tenant attracted, re-ordering of lease terms and duration to facilitate management, realization of potential including replacement of outworn buildings, acquisitions of adjoining property and any other steps likely to improve the holding or portfolio.

The report should be a dispassionate assessment of the position, giving alternative courses of action where available and pointing out the advantages and drawbacks of implementing a particular decision.

When the report has been discussed with the owner and his views and preferences ascertained, it will be possible to prepare a strategy towards the achievement of which the management effort will be directed. Following these discussions he should be in a position to set out a programme and a time scale. Any plan must be flexible because many of its parts will not be directly within the control of the owner but rather his preferred response in the event of certain happenings. In many cases it will be fruitful to repeat the exercise at suitable intervals.

4.5   DECISION MAKING

Until fairly recently the typical property manager saw his on-the-job training and subsequent experience as fitting him to undertake the specialism of property management. He regarded attempts to analyse and theorize his intuitive world with scepticism if not disdain and discounted formal training in contributing to finding the solution to a problem which was in all probability unique.

There is now more general recognition that scientific method can improve the quality of decision making. Recent developments in the practice of property investment and management have, by their sheer scale and increasing sophistication, convinced professional men that it is essential to break down decision making and planning into principles, the application of which will increase the probability of taking the best course of action.

But decisions rely on forecasts and no forecasting is without hazards, partly due to the absence of facts and partly to the effect of various external factors over which the decision maker has no control. The literature on this topic is formidable and the interested reader is referred to those specialized texts, a few of which are listed at the end of this chapter. The present intention is to do no more than outline the essential elements of and approach to decision making, with the complication that in most cases the property manager will be putting forward a recommendation only, the final decision being made by the client.

The role of the property manager is to provide his principal promptly with the necessary facts, opinions, alternatives and estimates of cost to enable the client to reach a sound decision. He should remember that he is an adviser only and the adoption of some course other than his recommended or preferred solution should not cause loss of objectivity or interest. Timing is often an important factor in obtaining a satisfactory response based on a logical rather than an emotional or intuitive approach and except where an urgent decision is necessary, he may consider delaying his recommendation to a more appropriate time where a delay will not prejudice the client's interests.

The adviser must make every effort to avoid bias and it may help to discuss his conclusions with a colleague before making recommendations. Similarly, he should seek help on any aspect of the problem on which he does not feel competent although he must pull the various strands together and take responsibility for the final proposals in order to take a positive role in any discussions with his client.

Finally, it is important that technical terms used by one party do not mislead the other. It may be necessary for the user to avoid such terms or to define what he intends his use of each term to convey.

4.6 WRITING REPORTS

In many cases, the adviser's recommendations will take the form of a report to his client. The cost of writing a report is substantial and every effort should be made to ensure that it achieves what it sets out to do.

Typically, the adviser will wish to confirm, inform and

advise his client and to obtain instructions. There may well be alternative courses of action available: it is no part of his task to persuade the client to take one route in preference to another but rather to set out the problem, the alternative solutions, the implications, the consequences and the financial commitment. He may even wish to set out solutions which, though impracticable, look attractive at first glance.

How best to do these things? The effectiveness of the report depends on the writer and his presentation. He must avoid complexity in what is often a complex subject: if he does not he may lose the attention of his reader. An excellent solution badly expressed is as unacceptable as a banal suggestion in faultless English.

He must show a thorough knowledge of the subject of his report: misinterpretation or misrepresentation will make serious inroads into his credibility as will flaws in his reasoning. If the report is not easy to read, it suffers the possibility of being ignored or misunderstood. New paragraphs, short sentences, proper headings and the relegation of detail to an appendix or schedule attached to the report will all assist in improving readability. Vagueness in expression and numbers should be avoided: percentages and ratios are often misused. Figures should be rounded off realistically to avoid a wrong inference of precision except where the figure may be ascertained exactly or is being quoted from another source.

A standard approach to the format of the report has much to commend it but care must be taken not to overlook any particular features which require comment in a particular case. On balance, summaries are best avoided as they tend to interfere with presentation of the recommendations for a certain course of action by influencing and misleading the reader.

Lastly, presentation of the report in a printed folder or binding, appropriately titled and well typed is no more than a good report deserves and will serve to give a favourable initial impression to the recipient.

FURTHER READING

Ratcliffe, J. (1976) *Land Policy*, Hutchinson, London.
Thomas, H. (1972) *Decision Theory and the Manager*, Pitman Publishing, London.

CHAPTER 5

Aspects of occupation

5.1 INTRODUCTION

The grant of an interest in land in exchange for periodic payment of a rent is a well developed commercial enterprise. The owner is enabled to receive a return on his capital while retaining a high degree of security and control over his investment.

The estate manager is centrally involved in various aspects of the transfer of limited interests in land. He negotiates the terms of the agreement between the parties, is responsible for their day to day interpretation and implementation during the currency of the arrangement and may be involved at the end of the period on questions such as dilapidations, fixtures and compensation for improvements. The purpose of this chapter is to provide a framework of understanding of the incidence of occupation so as to enable him to play his important role while at the same time recognizing the limitations of his appointment and training.

Prior to 1926, there were three complicated branches of law dealing with various aspects of real property. The provisions were long overdue for simplification and a committee was appointed with instructions to consider the existing position and to advise what action should be taken to facilitate and cheapen the transfer of land.

As a consequence, fundamental changes were introduced in 1926. There remains a degree of subtlety in the legislation and care is needed in the transfer of an interest in land to ensure that the required result is achieved.

These major structural alterations in the law should be distinguished from other provisions introduced at various times to modify certain aspects of contracts freely entered into, where the intention has been to balance the negotiating strengths of the parties (e.g. in the case of business tenancies) or to respond to current pressures and notions of fairness (e.g. enfranchisement of long leases). Elsewhere interference has been overtly political, as in the case of rent restriction, with the result that the provision of private rented accommodation is no longer regarded by investors as a sensible business activity.

5.2 LEASEHOLD INTERESTS

A lease confers a legal estate subject to it being created in accordance with the law and satisfying the statutory definition of a 'term of years' absolute in section 205(1) (xxvii) of the *Law of Property Act 1925*

> 'a term of years (taking effect either in possession or in reversion whether or not at a rent) with or without impeachment for waste, subject or not to another legal estate, and either certain or liable to determination by notice, re-entry, operation of law, or by a provision for cesser on redemption, or in any other event (other than the dropping of a life, or the determination of a determinable life interest); but does not include any term of years determinable with life or lives or with the cesser of a determinable life interest, nor, if created after the commencement of this Act, a term of years which is not expressed to take effect in possession within twenty-one years after the creation thereof where required by this Act to take effect within that period; and in the definition the expression "term of years" includes a term for less than a year, or for a year or years and a fraction of a year or from year to year'

while by (1) (ix) of the same section

> 'land includes land of any tenure, and mines and minerals, whether or not held apart from the surface, buildings or parts of buildings (whether the division is horizontal, vertical or made in any other way) and other corporeal hereditaments; also a manor, an advowson, and a rent and other incorporeal hereditaments, and an easement, right, privilege, or benefit in, over, or derived from land; but not an undivided share in land.'

A lease will never convey the landlord's entire interests in the land because that would be an assignment: it will always be for a term shorter than the landlord's interest, thus reserving a reversion, which may be substantial or a matter of as little as a day or so.

Possession must be exclusive; the expression 'possession' is a legal rather than a physical notion and thus extends beyond the popular meaning of the word to include the right to receive rents and profits arising out of the land. The landlord may reserve the right to enter, at certain times or on notice, for particular purposes.

Leases must with few exceptions be made by deed otherwise they are merely interests at will. The most important exception is of parol leases taking effect in possession for a term not exceeding three years, with or without power to the lessee to extend the term, at the best rent which can be reasonably obtained. A lease for longer than three years is not within the exception even though it may be determined within three years.

In all other cases, writing is required by section 40(1)

'No action may be brought upon any contract for the sale or other disposition of land or any interest in land, unless the agreement upon which such action is brought or some memorandum or note thereof, is in writing, and signed by the party to be charged or by some other person thereunto by him lawfully authorised'

The *Solicitors Act 1957* provides that any unqualified person who draws or prepares a lease for reward is guilty of a criminal offence. A parol lease is an agreement under hand and therefore not affected by this restriction.

There are a number of types of tenancy.

5.2.1   A term of years

At common law, a tenancy for a fixed period comes to an end at the expiration of that period but statute has introduced various restrictions on the right of the landlord to obtain possession against the wishes of his tenant.

The lease must be for a certain duration and must take

effect within 21 years of the date of the lease otherwise it is void. A lease for a life or lives takes effect as a lease for 90 years determinable by notice on death of the life or lives.

A lease may contain a covenant for renewal of the lease on its expiration: provision for a renewal for a term exceeding 60 years is void.

Where the covenant for renewal of the lease includes the renewal covenant in its entirety, it will be seen that the lease would be perpetually renewable. However, by statute such a provision will operate as an agreement to grant a lease for a term of 2000 years, though the right reserved to receive any fine (premium) on renewal will be lost. The tenant alone retains a right to terminate at the end of the original term by giving at least ten days' notice in writing.

5.2.2   From year to year

A tenancy from year to year is one which continues until determined by notice at the end of the first or any sub-sequent year and may be created by express grant or by necessary implication from the facts of occupation.

A letting stated to be at a yearly rent is likely to be a tenancy from year to year, even though 'there is a provision for payment of rent monthly, quarterly or at some other interval less than a year'.

5.2.3   For less than a year

A tenancy from week to week, month to month or other periods is similar to a tenancy from year to year except that the length of notice is related to the periodic interval. The parties may provide otherwise or the tenancy may be subject to statutory provisions as to the length of notice.

A month is a calendar month unless otherwise provided by the tenancy agreement.

5.2.4   At will

The courts are not anxious to infer a tenancy at will.

'It may be that the tenancy at will can now serve only one

legal purpose and that is to protect the interests of an occupier during a period of transition' (Heslop *v*. Burns 1974)

It is the lowest estate known to the law, being for no certain term and determinable at any time by the parties. It will determine automatically where either party dies, assigns his interest, gives notice or does some act inconsistent with such a tenancy. A tenancy at will is not usually created expressly. The parties may agree that no rent should be paid but otherwise the landlord is entitled to payment for use and occupation.

The tenant has the right to remove his goods from the premises within a reasonable time after the termination of the tenancy. Payment of rent at regular intervals will convert the tenancy into a periodic tenancy.

5.2.5 On sufferance

A tenant who remains in possession at the end of a fixed term without the consent of the landlord becomes a tenant on sufferance. The landlord may eject the tenant at any time and where the tenant wilfully remains in possession after written notice, he may become liable to pay double the yearly value.

Where rent is paid and accepted there may well be a presumption that the tenancy has become a periodic tenancy.

The difference between a tenancy at will and a tenancy on sufferance is that the latter exists without the landlord's consent.

Statutory provisions enabling residential and business tenants to continue in occupation after the expiration of the term and other modifications of the common law position are discussed elsewhere.

5.3 AGREEMENTS FOR LEASES

An agreement for a lease is a contract whereby one party binds himself to grant and the other binds himself to accept a lease at some future date.

Where there is any doubt as to whether the contract entered into is a lease or an agreement for a lease, the court will decide the issue by considering the intention of the parties and whether the document is complete in itself and intended to be acted on (a lease) or whether it contemplates a further stage (when it is likely to be regarded as an agreement for a lease).

The distinction is important. In the first place, a relaxation of the need for writing in respect of certain leases noted above does not apply to agreements for leases. The latter are governed by the provisions of section 40(1) which was quoted previously (p. 40). Secondly, an agreement for a lease followed by the tenant entering into possession and paying rent will operate only as a yearly tenancy regardless of the term contemplated by the contract between the parties. This may lead to complications in that some of the covenants incorporated in the original agreement may not be appropriate to a yearly tenancy. But it is expressly provided that failure to comply with the requirements of the Act shall not

> 'affect the right to acquire an interest in land by virtue of taking possession' (section 55(c))

Enforcement of the terms of the original contract may be possible where there has been a sufficient act of part performance. The leading case of Walsh *v.* Lonsdale 1882 decided that the tenant holds under the same terms in equity as if a lease had been granted: but as specific performance is a discretionary remedy there is always a possibility that it may not be granted in which case the tenant is thrown back on his common law position as a yearly tenant. An equitable lease is an estate contract and should be registered as a land charge under the *Land Charges Act 1972* otherwise it will be void against a *bona fide* purchaser of the legal estate for *value without notice*: notice means registration. Without registration a purchaser will not be bound by an agreement even though he is aware of it.

Where specific performance is not granted the remedy available to the injured party is an action for damages.

5.4 LEASES

Where writing is required by law, landlord and tenant enter

into a contract setting out the subject matter and the rights and duties of the parties. The contract is specifically an instrument under seal which conveys part of the landlord's interest to the tenant and which is referred to as a lease. One essential feature of a lease is that the landlord retains a reversion: in other words that he does not part with the whole of his interest. There is no prescribed form of lease and any appropriate words will be sufficient: nevertheless, most leases follow a settled pattern.

The simple purpose of a lease from the landlord's point of view is to regulate the tenant's occupation to the best advantage of the landlord, while the tenant has the benefit of knowing the precise terms — rights and obligations — of his temporary occupation.

The terms of the lease are sometimes negotiated between the parties but more often than not, one or both parties are represented by agents. When the parties are at one, their respective solicitors take over preparation of a draft lease. A small property let in its entirety is unlikely to create any major problems but the letting of a suite of offices in a large block or a shop unit in a mall of a modern shopping development will present the solicitors with problems of identity, grants and reservations of access, liability for a proportionate share of the cost of repairs, services and insurance and equality with other occupiers. To some extent such lettings tend towards a standard form of lease which, while highly desirable from a management point of view, may not be altogether satisfactory to the tenant.

Solicitors rarely view the premises with which they are concerned and it is important for the property manager to point out any peculiarities or features of the building which may require special provisions in the lease. Where a building is to be let in a number of parts, the essential terms need to be determined before the first letting takes place. This is an area where solicitor and agent can and should work together very closely to the benefit of their client and in the interests of efficient and responsible management.

It is always helpful for the property manager to provide a floor plan by means of which the significance of any requirements can often be more easily appreciated. Many solicitors now send a copy of the draft lease to the property manager as a matter of course for his comments and for confirmation that the intentions of the parties have been interpreted accurately.

The usual form of lease is divided into five parts —

The premises
The habendum
The reddendum
The covenants and provisions
The exceptions and reservations

while many modern leases are in a standard form, followed by schedules setting out details of parties and rent and other terms.

5.4.1 The premises

That part of the lease where the parties are named, the property to be let is identified and the broad intentions of the parties are expressed.

Except where there is no difficulty in identifying the precise extent of the premises, it may be helpful to include a plan or plans, especially where the demise consists of part of a larger building. Care must be taken to establish whether the written description or the plan takes precedence. Where the demise is part of a larger building there are likely to be rights and duties in relation to support, access, common facilities, services and utilities.

For the purpose of maintenance and calculation of service charges, the points of vertical and horizontal division are of practical importance. The landlord must except the external face of a wall if he wishes to make use of it for a purpose such as locating an advertisement.

5.4.2 The habendum

The date of commencement of the lease is fixed as is its duration.

The date of commencement of the lease must be fixed or be ascertainable at the time when the lease takes effect and the term must be certain.

It has been noted earlier that a lease must take effect

within 21 years of the date of the instrument creating it if it is to be valid. Certain classes of owner are limited as to the length of lease to be granted but otherwise a lease may be for whatever term the parties agree. A tenant in business premises will favour a long term to provide stability and protect his goodwill: the landlord, on the other hand, will be reluctant to grant such a term which will leave him progressively worse off in real terms as inflation continues. The market has developed to meet the reasonable requirements of both parties by the grant of a lease for a substantial term with provision for regular rent reviews, the most acceptable interval being 5 years though many leases provide a 7 year interval and an earlier bullish market achieved reviews at 3 year intervals.

The lease may contain a provision for either or both parties to determine (or break) the lease earlier than its declared termination. A right to determine on the part of the tenant only is unattractive to the landlord as it is likely to be operated only when economic circumstances are unfavourable. A more equitable alternative would be the grant of a shorter term and for the tenant to rely on the security of tenure provided by Part II of the *Landlord and Tenant Act 1954*. The residential tenant in general has considerable statutory protection.

It is the time honoured practice for a tenancy to commence on one of the usual quarter days (25 March, 24 June, 29 September and 25 December) although in certain parts of the country the traditional dates are 8 February, 9 May, 8 August and 11 November.

Many businessmen prefer payments to be made quarterly on the first of the month (1 March, 1 June, 1 September and 1 December) and modern leases often reflect this preference.

The tenant may negotiate an option to renew the tenancy for a further term, usually on similar terms to the existing lease except that the option to renew must be omitted from the new lease if the provisions of the *Law of Property Act 1922* converting the grant into a lease for a term of 2000 years are to be avoided.

An option to renew must be accompanied by provisions for determining the rent to be paid under the new lease if it is not to be void for uncertainty.

The use of options to renew is much less important now

that the business tenant has statutory rights to renew in the majority of cases.

5.4.3 The reddendum

That part of the lease which reserves the amount of rent and the manner in which it is to be paid, i.e. the interval of payment and whether in advance or in arrear of occupation. The provision that the amount of rent reserved by a lease must be certain caused some doubt to be expressed as to the enforceability of rent review clauses. It is now settled law that arrangements of this nature are valid provided there is some certain way in which the rent may be ascertained.

5.4.4 The covenant and provisions

A covenant is an agreement under seal and may be expressed or implied, positive or negative, real or personal. Express covenants are those set out in the deed whereas implied covenants are those which the law infers from the nature of the transaction as being necessary to its proper operation.

Real covenants are those which affect the nature, quality or value of the land. Subject to certain conditions, such covenants run with the land — that is to say the burden may be enforced and the benefit enjoyed by successors in title. Personal covenants are effective between the original parties only and do not run with the land. Covenants to repair, to insure and not to carry on a particular trade have all been held to be real covenants: an example of a personal covenant is an option to purchase.

The original parties to a lease are bound by its provisions for the whole of the term by virtue of the doctrine of privity of contract: this remains so even where the tenant assigns his lease or the landlord his reversion.

The law will imply the following covenants in the absence of any express provision:

on the part of the tenant:

(a) To pay the rent, in arrear unless otherwise provided: rent continues to be payable even if the property is destroyed
(b) To pay the usual rates and taxes

(c) To use the premises in a tenant-like manner
(d) To deliver up possession at the end of the term in the same condition, fair wear and tear excepted

and on the part of the landlord:

(a) To allow quiet enjoyment
(b) Not to derogate from his grant
(c) To give possession
(d) To pay landlord's taxes
(e) In the case of a furnished house, to ensure that it is fit for human habitation at the commencement of the tenancy

These covenants do not necessarily achieve the intentions of the parties and it is much more satisfactory to make specific provision.

The original parties to a lease are bound by its provisions for the whole of the term by virtue of the doctrine of privity of contract: this remains so even where the tenant assigns his lease or the landlord his reversion.

Where an assignment takes place there is no privity of contract but there is privity of estate between the party entitled to the lease and the party entitled to the reversion, provided that the covenant has reference to the subject matter of the lease.

Thus there is both privity of contract and privity of estate between the original parties. In the absence of a contractual relationship, there is privity of estate. Where the landlord assigns his reversion he will usually require an express covenant of indemnity: in the case of the tenant assigning his lease an indemnity covenant is implied by section 77 of the *Law of Property Act 1925.*

Unlike an original party to a lease, an assignee is liable only for breaches occurring while the interest is vested in him.

A covenant may be void because it requires or permits something which is illegal, immoral or impossible. Where it is feasible to separate that covenant from the contract, the contract will operate without it: otherwise the whole contract will be void.

It is now proposed to discuss some of the more usual covenants entered into by the parties.

(a) *To pay rent and other outgoings*

The provisions as to how and when the rent should be paid are contained in the reddendum: the covenant is an express undertaking by the tenant to pay the rent as provided. The modern tendency is to refer to any payments due from the tenant for insurance and other liabilities as 'additional rent'. There are two advantages to this arrangement: first, the landlord will be in a position to distrain on non-payment of any of the amounts and not be limited to the true rent payment: secondly, in the event of liquidation or bankruptcy of the tenant rent is a prior charge on the assets of the lessee, the additional security thus offered being another reason for the high standing of land and buildings as an investment.

(b) *To pay all rates, taxes and other outgoings*

The parties are in general at liberty to agree who is to be liable for outgoings, although this right is substantially curtailed in the case of residential property subject to the Rent Acts.

Unless there is a specific agreement to the contrary, drainage charges and the cost of abatement of nuisances are payable by the owner. Where there is no agreement and the costs are recovered in the first instance from the tenant, he is entitled to deduct the amount from future rent.

Such covenants are often drawn very widely to ensure that the landlord will not be responsible for any outgoings ('even though of a wholly novel character' as one precedent has it). A modern response to the rating of empty premises is to provide specifically for the tenant to pay any empty rate or rating surcharge.

(c) *User*

A lease may make no mention of the use to which premises are to be put in which case the tenant has freedom to pursue any use within the law.

The more common position is that some provisions are made as to user. The tenant may be limited to a particular use or prohibited from engaging in a particular specified use but be free to engage in any other use. The implications of any limitation on the rental value of the premises should

be considered in relation to the benefits to be gained by the
landlord from the restriction. The intention may be to retain
some control over the type of trade carried on, in that the
tenant will not be able to make any change without first
applying to the landlord for permission: it may be intended
to benefit occupiers of a number of properties all belonging
to the same landlord by restricting competition in the immediate locality. Current retail practice does not favour
strict demarcations of this nature. Where the landlord carries
on a business, he may wish to restrict competition from
nearby premises in his ownership.

The effect of user covenants on the rental value of business
premises on review during the currency of a lease and also on
renewal by the court under the 1954 legislation is discussed
in Chapter 7. The landlord will seek to prevent the tenant
from engaging in any noxious or offensive use of the premises.

By section 19(3) of the *Landlord and Tenant Act 1927*
any covenant against the alteration of user without licence
or consent shall, where no structural alteration is involved,
be deemed to be subject to a proviso that no fine or sum
of money in the nature of a fine shall be payable in respect
of such a licence or consent. The landlord is not thereby
precluded from requiring payment of a reasonable sum in
respect of any damage to or diminution in the value of the
premises or any neighbouring premises belonging to him and
of any legal or other expenses incurred.

A lease of a dwelling-house commonly contains a covenant
restricting occupation to use as a dwelling-house with a prohibition against use for any illegal or immoral purpose or
any purpose likely to annoy or disturb the landlord, his
tenants or the occupiers of adjoining properties.

Many modern leases seek to ensure that retail premises
forming part of a shopping centre development open for
trading by providing minimum or standard opening hours.
The requirements should be able to accommodate late
night shopping at a supermarket, five-day trading by banks
and some other occupiers of retail units and the custom
adopted by some florists, greengrocers, fishmongers and
others of closing all day on a Monday.

The trading hours provision is valuable to the landlord,
particularly where a shopping development is not success-

ful for one reason or another. From the tenant's point of view the prospect of paying not only the rent but also the trading overheads is particularly onerous where the trading position of the premises has deteriorated to the point of becoming uneconomic. The individual tenant would be unlikely to survive for long whereas the public company retailer could withstand the cost indefinitely.

(d) *Not to assign or underlet*

The tenant is usually required to undertake not to assign or underlet the whole or any part of the premises. Frequently the restriction is qualified by the addition of words such as 'without the written consent of the landlord' while a further relaxation is often granted by the use of a form of words providing that 'such consent however not to be unreasonably withheld'.

An absolute prohibition operates precisely as that, whereas a qualified prohibition is subject to section 19(1) of the *Landlord and Tenant Act 1927* which provides that

'In all leases whether made before or after the commencement of this Act containing a covenant condition or agreement against assigning, under-letting, charging or parting with the possession of demised premises or any part thereof without licence or consent, such covenant condition or agreement shall, notwithstanding any express provision to the contrary, be deemed to be subject —

(a) to a proviso to the effect that such licence or consent is not to be unreasonably withheld, but this proviso does not preclude the right of the landlord to require payment of a reasonable sum in respect of any legal or other expenses incurred in connection with such licence or consent; and

(b) (if the lease is for more than forty years, and is made in consideration wholly or partially of the erection, or the substantial improvement, addition or alteration of buildings, and the lessor is not a Government department or local or public authority, or a statutory or public utility company) to a proviso to the effect that in the case of any assignment, under-letting, charging or parting with the possession (whether by the holders of the lease or any under-tenant whether immediate or not) effected more than seven years before the end of the term no consent or licence shall be required, if notice in writing of the transaction is given to the lessor within six months after the transaction is effected.'

Where the lease makes no reference to assignment or sub-letting the tenant is entitled to assign or sub-let the premises. Where the tenant assigns he transfers the whole of his remaining interest in the premises to another person, known as the assignee, who takes on the role of the original tenant in respect of covenants that touch and concern the land in accordance with the doctrine of privity of estate. Such covenants are enforceable by or against him. By section 77(1) of the *Law of Property Act 1925* an indemnity by the assignee is implied in favour of the assignor in relation to any future breaches of covenant.

A legal assignment must be effected by deed in accordance with the provisions of section 52(1) of the *Law of Property Act 1925* regardless of the status of the original letting. An assignment not by deed operates as an equitable assignment. A sub-letting merely creates another tier in the landlord—tenant relationship: the new tenant is responsible to his immediate landlord who, as tenant, remains responsible to the superior landlord. The statutory modifications imposed on assignment and sub-lettings of residential properties will be discussed in Chapter 8.

(e) *To repair and maintain*

The responsibility for repairs should be detailed as in the absence of express provision neither party will be fully responsible and the position will be very unsatisfactory. In certain circumstances, the landlord is unable to shift the burden of repair onto the tenant (see, for example, the repair burden placed on the landlord by section 32 of the *Housing Act 1961* which provides specifically that

'... any covenant by the lessee for the repair of the premises ... shall be of no effect so far as it relates to the matters mentioned in paragraphs (a) and (b) of this sub-section')

(f) *Not to carry out alterations or improvements*

A restriction on carrying out alterations is an important safeguard for the landlord in ensuring that the premises do not lose their identity or the structure suffer physical distress. A covenant may be absolute, in which case the landlord's refusal is final. Where the covenant is qualified to the extent that alterations are prohibited except with the consent of the landlord, it is implied by the *Landlord and Tenant Act 1927* that such consent is not to be unreasonably withheld in the case of improvements. In this extended form, any alteration which is an improvement is subject to provisions contained in the *Landlord and Tenant Act 1927* that such consent may not be unreasonably withheld. It is not possible to contract out of this provision. Where the landlord refuses consent in spite of this proviso, the tenant may apply to the court for permission.

The court will not grant permission to the tenant where the landlord agrees to undertake the work in consideration of a reasonable rent.

Compliance with the procedure for service of notice with plans and specifications is essential if the tenant is to establish the basis of his right to compensation for the improvement on quitting.

Improvements required by the landlord as a condition of granting a lease will not be the subject of compensation when the tenant leaves. It is common to stipulate that such improvements together with any alterations for which the landlord gives his consent are to be reinstated at the landlord's option at the end of the lease. The landlord then has the opportunity to consider whether the work is of any benefit to his reversion: it may also enable him to argue that the tenant's expenditure has not involved the landlord in any benefit and thus avoid the problem of tax on a notional premium equal to the increase in the value of his reversion.

(g) *To comply with statutory notices*

The usual form of the covenant is designed to place the burden of complying with legislation and statutory notices served thereunder on the tenant. Notices may affect the premises or the trade or business carried on therein. The use of premises for purposes as diverse as selling gunpowder or pets requires to be registered or licensed. Some of the more common requirements are summarized below.

Much recent legislation has been concerned with standards in buildings for the benefit of occupiers, whether as tenants or employees, and various third parties.

Occupiers' Liability Act 1957

This is among the more important enactments. Any occupier of premises owes a duty of care to visitors so that they will be reasonably safe in their lawful use of the premises. The landlord will be responsible as the occupier in respect of any part of the building, such as common parts, over which he retains control. He may attempt to limit or exclude his liability by agreement or other means, provided that any changes can be shown to be reasonable: he cannot however exclude or restrict liability for death or personal injury.

He is not liable to trespassers except that he must not deliberately set out to inflict injury. Unless he has taken every care to exclude children as trespassers, he may have a greater liability to this category.

Offices Shops and Railway Premises Act 1963

The broad purpose of the Act is to provide a minimum standard of working accommodation for employees. Provision is made for the landlord or tenant to apply to the County Court to apportion the expenses incurred. Where the work required is contrary to provisions contained in the lease, application may be made to the County Court to make the necessary modifications to the lease.

Fire Precautions Act 1971

Subject to minor exceptions the Act provides that use of premises for the purposes of a factory, office, shop or railway premises where persons are employed requires the issue of a fire certificate.

There are requirements for a current fire certificate to be held at the premises.

Where the premises are in multi-occupation, the owner is responsible for compliance with the regulations.

Defective Premises Act 1972
The Act places on a landlord a duty of care to all persons who might reasonably be expected to be affected by defects in the state of premises. He is required to see that they are reasonably safe from personal injury or from damage to their property caused by a relevant defect. The duty is owed where the landlord knows of the relevant defect because he has been notified by the tenant or if he ought to have known of it in all the circumstances. A 'relevant defect' is defined as a defect arising out of a breach by the landlord of his repairing obligations.

Health and Safety at Work Act 1974
The Act made provision for the introduction of regulations designed to reduce accidents and bad working conditions. The provisions are concerned largely with the relationship between employer and employee, their respective duties and the formal framework to ensure that a statement policy is prepared and implemented.

Other legislation concerning the standard or use of premises includes

> *Explosives Act 1875*
> *Alkali Works Regulation Act 1906*
> *Petroleum (Consolidation) Act 1928*
> *Shops Act 1950*
> *Fireworks Act 1951*
> *Food and Drugs Act 1955*
> *Clean Air Acts 1956* and *1968*
> *Guard Dogs Act 1975*
> *Factories Act 1961* and
> *Town and Country Planning Acts 1947—1971*

(h) *To insure*
The essentials of the covenant to insure are that the premises are covered for the usual risks (loss or damage by fire, explosion, flood, lightning and aircraft), the cover is for the full replacement cost together with fees, the payments are main-

tained up to date, the receipt is produced to the landlord on demand and that in the event of loss or damage the premises are reinstated without delay and to the reasonable satisfaction of the landlord, any shortfall in insurance monies being made up by the tenant.

Alternatively, the landlord may effect insurance cover and claim the premium from the tenant as additional rent. In modern developments containing numerous occupiers, it is appropriate for the landlord to insure the whole in which case there will be no need to define individual tenant's responsibilities with regard to parts of the structure, common passages, staircases and so on. Careful consideration must be given to additional cover required by any tenant by virtue of any special or unusual risk.

Loss of rent for the estimated period of rebuilding is usually included in the cover.

At common law the tenant is liable to pay rent even where the property has been destroyed. Specific provision should therefore be made for abatement of rent during the period of rebuilding: partial destruction should be treated on a *pro rata* basis.

(i) *To pay service charges*

Where the premises let to the tenant are part of a larger development such as a block of offices or a shopping centre, it is likely that charges directly and indirectly attributable to occupation will be collected by way of a service charge.

The charge will include payments in respect of insurance, the landlord's obligations to repair, redecorate, cleanse and maintain, general and water rates and the cleansing, lighting and general maintenance of the common facilities, supervision and management of the development and the cost of compliance with statutes, rules and regulations. The covenant may also provide for the apportionment of the cost of promotional or other work carried out at the request of a majority of the tenants for the benefit of the development as a whole.

The amount of the service charge will be ascertained and certified annually by the landlord or his managing agents or his accountants. Apportionment may be by means of floor area, rateable value or use by a combination of these methods or by weighting various aspects.

Large sums may be involved in providing the various services and provision is often made for a payment in advance on account of the estimated costs for the ensuing three months. Service charges payable in respect of residential accommodation are subject to strict control as explained in Chapter 9.

(j) *To surrender*

The lease usually contains a specific covenant on the part of the tenant to surrender and yield up possession of the premises in good repair and condition at the end or sooner determination of the term.

(k) *Costs, fees and stamp duty*

The tenant may be required to pay the landlord's costs of preparing and executing the lease and counterpart together with the stamp duty payable. Such an agreement cannot be enforced unless it meets the requirements of the *Cost of Leases Act 1958*. The Act provides that, notwithstanding any custom to the contrary a party to a lease shall be under no obligation to pay the other party's costs of the lease unless the parties thereto agree otherwise in writing.

Costs are defined to include fees, charges, disbursements including stamp duty, expenses and remuneration.

Provision is usually made for the tenant to reimburse the landlord for all solicitors' and surveyors' fees and disbursements in connection with notices under section 146 or 147 of the *Law of Property Act 1925* or on any application by the tenant for a consent or licence required under the leases.

(l) *Landlord's covenants*

The usual covenants by the landlord are for quiet enjoyment, to maintain and repair those parts of the demised premises for which he is responsible together with the common areas and where appropriate to insure and to apply all insurance monies to rebuilding.

(m) *Provisos*

The lease usually continues with a series of provisos setting

out in some detail the agreement between the parties in the
event of certain eventualities.

(i) Forfeiture and re-entry

A lease is liable to forfeiture where the tenant breaches
a condition of his lease or breaks a covenant but in the latter
case only where the lease contains an express provision for
forfeiture.

Where the breach concerns the non-payment of rent the
landlord must bring an action for recovery following termination of the tenancy. Forfeiture may be waived by any act by
the landlord which is inconsistent with forfeiture. Payment
into court of all arrears of rent and costs has the effect of
staying proceedings and enables the tenant to apply to the
court for relief which is entirely in the discretion of the court.
A sub-tenant may seek relief against forfeiture of the tenant's
interest. Forfeiture for breach of any other covenant is
governed by the provisions of section 146 of the *Law of
Property Act 1925* which provides, in part

'(1) A right of re-entry or forfeiture under any proviso
or stipulation in a lease for a breach of any covenant or
condition in the lease shall not be enforceable, by action
or otherwise, unless and until the lessor serves on the
lessee a notice —

(a) specifying the particular breach complained of: and
(b) if the breach is capable of remedy, requiring the lessee
to remedy in the breach; and
(c) in any case requiring the lessee to make compensation
in money for the breach;

and the lessee fails, within a reasonable time thereafter, to
remedy the breach, if it is capable of remedy, and to make
reasonable compensation in money, to the satisfaction of
the lessor, for the breach.'

It is provided that the section has effect notwithstanding any
stipulation to the contrary.

The court has power to grant relief from forfeiture and if
it does so may give a direction for costs and compensation
as it thinks fit.

As in the case of non-payment of rent, forfeiture may be

waived by an inconsistent act of the landlord. However, in the case of continuing breaches of covenant, waiver applies only to those breaches having taken place and subsequent breaches offer the landlord a further opportunity to enforce a forfeiture.

It is usual to require the tenant to undertake to pay costs incurred by the landlord in the service of notices under section 146.

(ii) Options

The lease may contain options available to the landlord, the tenant, or with both parties to the lease.

There may be an option for either or both parties to determine or bring the lease to an end on a date prior to that specified in the lease. The option to determine may stand alone or be associated with a rent review clause, the intention then being to give the tenant an opportunity to discontinue the lease where, for example, the new rent level is not acceptable to him or where a limited planning permission has come to an end and not been renewed.

An option to renew the lease at the expiration of the term is less frequent now that the tenant has considerable security of tenure under the *Landlord and Tenant Act 1954*. Nevertheless, it remains a valuable right for the tenant as it precludes the landlord serving a statutory notice and citing one of the grounds provided by the Act in support of his refusal to grant a new tenancy.

An option to renew should deal with the time and manner in which it should be exercised and set out the terms of the lease. It may be provided that the new lease is in the same form as the existing one, save that the amount of rent payable will be subject to alteration.

The covenant for renewal should not be repeated, otherwise the effect would be to create a perpetually renewable lease which would operate as a demise for 2000 years.

It may be thought that the defendant landlord in Marjorie Burnett Ltd *v.* Barclay was slightly fortunate. A lease containing an option to renew for a further seven years contained the further proviso that

'. . . such lease shall also contain a like covenant for

renewal for a further term of seven years on the expiration
of the term thereby granted'

It was held that this clause was not part of the covenant for
renewal.

An option for renewal is an estate contract registrable as a
Class C (iv) charge under section 2(4) of the *Land Charges
Act 1972*. In the event of non-registration the option is void
against an assignee for money or money's worth (Midland
Bank Trust Co Ltd *v*. Green).

Finally, the lease may contain an option to purchase in
favour of the tenant.

The option should state the conditions to be observed in
its exercise and either specify a price or give instructions as to
its determination.

The option must be exercised as provided. Unless expressly
provided to the contrary, an option will not survive termination of the lease.

Again, the option should be registered. In a recent case,
it was held that an option to purchase the reversion at a
valuation was ineffective because the landlords declined to
appoint a valuer to agree the price with the tenants' valuer.
Templeton L. J., giving the judgment of the court, said

'We arrive at that conclusion regretfully because the option
was clearly intended to be effective and was at the time
thought to be effective . . . Nevertheless, it seems to us
that . . . the parties succeeded in selecting a classically
uncertain form which the court cannot assist them to
operate' (Sudbrook Trading Estate Ltd *v*. Eggleton and
Others 1981)

(iii) Service of notices
Provision is often made for the service of notices, by stipu-
lating an address to which any notice must be delivered.
Where there is a subsequent change of address, service should
probably be made to both addresses. The form of notice may
be specified but will be overridden by forms of notice prescribed by statute.

(iv) Settlement of disputes
The most likely cause of dispute under a lease with provisions

for periodic reviews of rent within the lease period is the amount of rent to be paid.

The provisions for initiating the review may be very detailed: the lease will lay down the procedure for resolving any failure of the parties to reach agreement. The common arrangement is for the appointment of an appropriate person to act as an arbitrator or as an independent valuer. The lease may provide for the President of the Royal Institution of Chartered Surveyors to make the appointment. Invariably, he will appoint a chartered surveyor who, in addition to the primary duty of making a determination of value, may be called upon to interpret aspects of law. The Institution has provided guidance notes for the assistance of arbitrators, independent valuers, the parties and those advising them.

The notes distinguish between an arbitrator and an independent valuer and proceed to discuss the appointment, acceptance, powers and duties of the appointee, the procedure before during and after the hearing or the receipt of written representations, the form of the Award and the treatment of fees and costs.

An arbitrator will be subject to the provisions of the *Arbitration Acts 1950* and *1979* but is not liable for negligence. The independent valuer makes use of his own knowledge in reaching a decision and *is* liable for negligence.

The case of Belvedere Motors Ltd *v.* King 1981 is a recent example of a charge of negligence being made by an aggrieved party against the independent valuer. The judgment by Jones J. shows a very clear understanding of the valuation issues and highlights the careful and thorough way in which the defendant went about his duties. The restatement of the applicable law is well worth reading in the full report.

(v) Schedules

Modern leases of premises within a development tend to be drawn in a standard form which is facilitated by the provision of several schedules dealing with aspects applicable to the particular property and setting out in detail a description of the demised premises, easements rights and privileges granted, exceptions and reservations, rules, regulations, services and charges, rents, term, revision years and the machinery for undertaking a review of rent including provision for settling disputes by arbitration or otherwise where the parties fail to reach an agreement.

5.5   LICENCES

A licence is a personal privilege which does not confer an interest in land, does not depend on exclusive possession and simply permits the licensee to do what would otherwise be a trespass.

A bare licence is one granted without valuable consideration. It cannot be assigned, may be revoked at any time and will be determined automatically if the owner of the property dies or conveys his interest to another.

The owner of the land may maintain an action of trespass against a former licensee remaining after revocation of his licence.

Where there is no specific provision for notice to terminate the licence, the law will imply whatever length of time is fair and reasonable between the parties.

A licence coupled with an interest in land (e.g. the right to enter the property of another and cut and remove turf) may be assigned unless otherwise agreed and in general is irrevocable during the currency of the interest.

It is unlikely that a mere licensee would be held liable to repair.

In an arrangement between an oil company and the operator of a filling station owned by the company, it was held that an agreement under which the grantor retained rights of possession and control over the property were consistent only with the grant of a licence: the grantee was therefore unable to claim protection as a business tenant under the *Landlord and Tenant Act 1954.*

The use of licences as a means of avoiding the provisions of the Rent Acts relating to security of tenure has been thoroughly explored by landlords and others and will be considered in Chapter 8.

5.6   RENTCHARGES

5.6.1   Introduction

A rentcharge may be defined as an annual or other periodic sum charged on or issuing out of land where the owner has no reversion in the land but has power to distrain either by express provision in the instrument creating the charge or by statute.

A rent reserved by a lease or any sum payable by way of mortgage is not a rentcharge.

The Law Commission considered the effect of the creation of rentcharges and reported a widely held view that the creation of rentcharges invaded the principle of freehold tenure with the sole purpose of providing a bonus for the builder: they concluded that the system required, at the very least, radical reform. As a result a private member's bill was introduced and received government support in its passage through Parliament to become the *Rentcharges Act 1977*.

5.6.2   Effect of Rentcharges Act 1977

The *Rentcharges Act* was passed to prohibit the creation and provide for the extinguishment apportionment and redemption of all but very limited types of rentcharge, the only two of any practical importance being the estate rentcharge and the variable rentcharge.

(a) *Estate rentcharges*

A rentcharge created for the purpose

(i) Of making covenants to be performed by the owner of the land affected by the rentcharge enforceable by the rent owner against the owner for the time being of the land or

(ii) Of meeting, or contributing towards, the cost of the performance by the rent owner of covenants for the provision of services, the carrying out of maintenance or repairs, the effecting of insurance or the making of any payment by him for the benefit of the land affected by the rentcharge or for that or other land shall be an estate rentcharge not subject to the provisions for redemption provided it is nominal in amount or unless it represents a reasonable amount for the performance by the rent owner of any covenant referred to in (i) above.

(b) *Variable rentcharges*

A rentcharge may be variable where the amount payable is related to some index and therefore not known in advance, or where the deed creating the rentcharge makes provision for variations to take effect at certain times in the future. In either case, the Act will not affect this class of rentcharge until it ceases to be variable, which time is to be regarded as the date on which the rentcharge became payable for the purpose of extinguishment.

5.6.3   Provision for extinguishment

The Act provides simply that every rentcharge other than those within the exclusions referred to shall be extinguished at the expiry of the period of 60 years beginning on 22 August 1977 or with the date on which the rentcharge first became payable, whichever is the later.

5.6.4   Provision for redemption

Where the rentcharge is not an estate rentcharge or one covered by the other limited exceptions, the rentchargee may apply to the Secretary of State to ascertain the sum payable and in due course to issue a redemption certificate on proof that the redemption price has been paid to the rentcharge owner or paid into court where the owner is not known.

Calculation of redemption price

The Act contains a formula for the calculation of the redemption price which relates the price to the current return on 2½% Consolidated Stock.

The formula is

$$P = \pounds\frac{R}{Y} - \frac{R}{Y(1 + Y)^n}$$

where

P = the redemption price
R = the annual rentcharge

Y = the yield, expressed as a decimal fraction, of 2½ per cent Consolidated Stock

n = the period in years for which the rentcharge would remain payable if it were not redeemed, any part of a year being taken as a year

Example

What is the redemption price for a rentcharge of £15 per annum payable in perpetuity where instructions for redemption are served by the Secretary of State on 19 March 1981?

Calculation

The yield is to be calculated on the middle market price at the close of business on the last trading day in the preceding week, i.e. 13 March 1981. The number of years is $(1977 + 60) - 1981 = 56$ years. The yield is calculated by dividing the nominal price by the middle market price and multiplying by 2.5 (the nominal interest rate). In this example the middle market price was £20.75 thus

$$\text{Yield} = \frac{100}{20.75} \times 2.5 = 12.048\%$$

or, as a decimal fraction

0.12048

Then

$$P = \frac{15}{0.12048} - \frac{15}{0.12048(1.12048)^{56}}$$

$$= £124.502 - £0.213$$

Redemption price = £124.29

The same result would be obtained by multiplying the annual rentcharge by the appropriate years' purchase table on the single rate basis.

There is no time limit for commencing the redemption procedure: the right is a continuing one and the time of redemption is reflected in the formula for calculation of the redemption price.

There are provisions enabling the Secretary of State to apportion a rentcharge not subject to redemption as between different owners of land or different parts of land in one ownership. Such apportionments are subject to a right of appeal to the Lands Tribunal.

Applicants for redemption or apportionment must bear their own expenses and the reasonable expenses of a mortgagee incurred in producing documents of title to the Secretary of State.

5.7 EASEMENTS AND PROFITS A *PRENDRE*

5.7.1 Easements

An easement is a right in *alieno solo* (in the soil of another) attached to the ownership of land and being a right to use or restrict the use of the other land. Examples are rights of way (a right to use) and rights of support and light (rights to restrict use).

The essential characteristics of an easement are that there must be a dominant and a servient tenement and the dominant and servient owners must be different persons: the easement must benefit the dominant tenement and the right must be capable of being granted by deed.

An easement is a legal easement if acquired by express, implied or presumed grant or granted by deed for an estate in fee simple absolute in possession or a term of years absolute in which case the benefit will pass to any later purchaser of the land. Where the easement has been created in any other way, it will be an equitable easement, enforceable against a purchaser of the legal estate in the servient tenement only if registered as a land charge. A public right is not an easement because it can be exercised by the public at large and is not dependent upon the ownership of land.

An owner may be prepared to grant an easement in or over his land. But he may be anxious that an adjoining owner does not acquire by long user any right which might restrict the present enjoyment of future development of the land. The property manager will use whatever means are available to prevent the acquisition of easements. For example, the owner who crosses his neighbour's yard as a short cut to his orchard should be prevented from doing so or requested to make an appropriate acknowledgement. Or the owner may bring an action for trespass. Some easements, for example of light or support, are likely to be acquired in time because usually there is no practical way in which to obstruct their enjoyment and their use does not involve a trespass.

An owner has a natural right of support against his neighbour or the owner of the subsoil held apart from the surface unless excluded by agreement or statute. However, the right dos not extend to a building, either by adjoining land or by an attached building. The right may be acquired by user after a period of enjoyment. Where physically connected buildings have been constructed at the same time by the same building owner, each conveyance could be expected to contain reciprocal grants and reservations.

5.7.2   Profits *à prendre*

A profit, like an easement or a rentcharge, is an incorporeal hereditament. It is a right to take certain limited things from the land of another (the servient tenement).

It is not necessary for there to be a dominant tenement but, in most cases where there is, the right is described as a profit appurtenant. Where there is no dominant tenement it is a profit in gross.

Profits exist as the right to take something from the soil itself (e.g. sand or gravel) or the produce of the soil (e.g. to pasture one's cattle or to take fish).

A profit may be acquired in similar ways to those described for easements, except that a profit in gross cannot be acquired by statutory prescription.

5.7.3   Extinguishment

Both easements and profits may be extinguished by release, either express or implied: by abandonment (not merely non-user), by operation of law or by unity of ownership and possession.

5.8   PUBLIC RIGHTS

A public right is a right enjoyed by the public at large which does not depend on ownership of land. The most common public right is a right of way.

A public right of way may be created by statute or by dedication and acceptance, usually inferred.

The *Highways Act 1959* provides that a right of way is deemed to have been dedicated where it has been enjoyed as of right by the public for twenty years or a shorter period where it can be shown that there was an intention to dedicate. Interruption of the use will defeat a claim. This may be physical, for example by closing the way once a year, or may be achieved by exhibiting a notice on or close to the way or by depositing a map with the local council and renewing it by means of a statutory declaration every six years.

It should be noted that the soil beneath the public right of way or highway remains vested in the adjoining owners.

Should the road cease to be a public highway, the land will revert to the adjoining owners. A practical example of such a case occurred when, as part of a pedestrianization scheme in a shopping street, a local authority proceeded to stop up a side street under powers contained in the *Highways Act*. The adjoining owners were able to combine and benefit to the extent of £250000 by selling the freehold in the former highway as the site for a shop development.

FURTHER READING

Baker, P. V. (1975) *A Manual of the Law of Real Property*, Stevens and Sons, London.

Burns, E. H. (1976) *Cheshire's Modern Law of Real Property*, Butterworths, London.

Curzon, L. B. (1979) *Land Law*, Macdonald and Evans, Plymouth.

CHAPTER 6

Business tenancies

6.1 INTRODUCTION

Nowadays it is a commonplace for the law to intervene to modify a contract, in order to afford a degree of protection to one of the parties to it. But it was not at all common when the *Landlord and Tenant Act* was passed in 1927, its main purpose being to give the tenant a right to a new lease or to some measure of compensation where a new lease was not available.

A majority report of a government appointed Leasehold Committee discerned a widely held belief that a landlord and tenant were unable to bargain from a position of equality and that the balance was heavily in favour of the landlord in spite of the intentions and provisions of the 1927 Act. The recommendations of the Committee sought to buffer the worst effects of the landlord's ability to obtain possession of premises occupied by a tenant and resulted eventually in the passing of the *Landlord and Tenant Act 1954*, Part II especially of which applies to business tenancies. This Act remains as the principal act though the *Law of Property Act 1969* made some improvements in its operation and effect: the 1927 Act survives only in respect of the provisions relating to compensation for improvements carried out by the tenant and this subject to modifications contained in the 1954 Act.

Some parts of the legislation have generated much litigation, especially over the last fifteen years or so, but in general the code has worked well and proved acceptable to both landlord and tenant. The tenant has enjoyed a considerable degree of security of tenure, with provisions for compensation where he has been required to vacate the premises against his wishes under certain rights of repossession reserved to the landlord in cases where the correctness of the tenant's conduct has not been in question. At the same time, the landlord has retained freedom to include in the lease agreed provisions for the review of the level of rent payable during the currency of the lease. The success of the statutory intervention may best be judged by the high level of activity in the investment market in business premises and by the acceptance of relatively low initial returns on such an investment.

Indeed, it is doubtful whether the landlord and tenant relationship in business premises could have developed without a framework of the kind now in force: without the confidence instilled by the legislation, many tenants would have sought to avoid the risks inherent in a free market by acquiring freehold premises — perhaps then much of the major commercial and industrial development of recent years would not have taken place.

The purpose of this chapter is to examine the precise, sometimes tedious but always important provisions of current legislation and the pronouncements of the courts. Consideration of the crucial area of rent reviews is dealt with in the following chapter.

The property manager plays a key role in regulating business tenancies and is unable to manage and negotiate rent reviews and renewals of leases without a proper grasp of the underlying statutory provisions and the case law flowing therefrom.

6.2 DEFINITIONS

Part II of the *Landlord and Tenant Act 1954* as amended by Part I of the *Law of Property Act 1969* applies

'. . . to any tenancy where the property comprised in the tenancy is or includes premises which are occupied by the tenant and are so occupied for the purposes of a business carried on by him or for those and other purposes' (section 23(1))

It is necessary to consider the several parts of this provision with help from the Act and from decisions of the courts.

First, it must be emphasized that a tenant who does not occupy or a tenant who occupies but does not carry on a business, is not afforded protection under the provisions of this part of the Act.

6.2.1   Tenancy

'Tenancy' means a tenancy created by a lease, underlease, agreement for a lease or an underlease or by a tenancy agreement but excludes certain types of lease and does not include a mortgage term or any interest in favour of a mortgagor arising from an attornment clause.

6.2.2   Premises

The courts have given a wide interpretation to the word 'premises' so as to extend to property other than buildings. For example, sand let to be used as gallops was held *not* to be an agricultural holding (as claimed) and was not therefore excluded from the provisions of Part II of the Act (Bracey *v.* Read 1963). On the other hand, it was held that a right of way was not and never could be within Part II as being occupied for the purposes of a business. (Land Reclamation Co. Ltd *v.* Basildon District Council 1978). Nor was an easement or something akin thereto (Jones *v.* Christy 1963).

6.2.3   Occupation

The tenant cannot claim security of tenure where he has sub-let the whole of the premises. Where he has sub-let only part, remaining in occupation of the other part, he is entitled to security in respect of that part of which he remains in occupation. Where the landlord requires the new tenancy to comprise the whole of the property included in the current tenancy, the tenant cannot seek a new tenancy only of that part which he occupies.

6.2.4   Business

The expression 'business' includes a trade, profession or employment and any activity carried on by a body of persons

whether corporate or unincorporate (section 23(2)). But
where the tenant is carrying on a business in breach of a
prohibition of use for business purposes (as distinct from a prohibition of use for the purposes of a *specified* business
or of any but a specified business) the premises will be excluded from the provisions of the Act unless the immediate
landlord or his predecessor in title has consented to the
breach or the immediate landlord has acquiesced therein.
The courts have had many opportunities to consider the
question of what constitutes a business.

A much quoted definition is that business

> 'means almost anything which is an occupation as dis-
> tinguished from a pleasure: anything which is an occupa-
> tion or a duty which requires attention . . . ' Lindley L. J.
> in Rolls *v.* Miller 1884).

The term has been held to include a tenancy of a tennis
club (Addiscombe Garden Estates Ltd *v.* Crabbe 1958):
premises let to a Minister 'for and on behalf of Her Majesty'
were held to be occupied by the Crown for the purposes of
a business carried on by the Crown (Town Investments Ltd *v.*
Department of the Environment 1977). Premises occupied to
carry on a seasonal business (Artemiou *v.* Procopiou 1965)
and the activities of the governors of a hospital in adminis-
tering the premises (Hills (Patents) Ltd *v.* University College
Hospital 1956) were both held to be occupied for the purposes of a business.

A sub-letting may be a business but it is protected only if
the tenant occupies (Bagettes *v.* G. P. Estates Co. Ltd. 1956).

Premises where the tenant occupied part as his residence,
sub-letting the remainder for business use and providing
various services were held to be occupied for the purposes
of a business and thus protected (Lee-Verhulst (Investments)
Ltd *v.* Harwood Trust).

It is not necessary for the business to be carried on at the
premises for Part II of the Act to apply to the tenancy: the
requirement is that it is occupied for the purposes of a
business: it is thought that a lock-up garage used to store a
van used in a business would be within the provisions of the
Act. But where a hotel owner took a tenancy of premises to
accommodate staff employed in his hotel it was held not to

be within the provisions of the Act as it was not necessary for the staff to live there and convenience was insufficient (Chapman *v.* Freeman 1978).

A tenant who used premises to conduct a Sunday School for one hour each week was held not to be carrying on a business (Abernethie *v.* A. M. and J. Kleiman 1970).

6.2.5 Holding

The term is applied to the premises comprised in the tenancy, excluding any part which is not occupied either by the tenant or by a person employed by him for the purposes of a business. It should be noted that the tenant does not have to occupy the whole of the premises for business purposes, but if he does so occupy any part, any other part occupied by him for other purposes (e.g. as living accommodation) is also entitled to the protection available under the Act.

6.2.6 Landlord

The description 'landlord' may be qualified by one of three adjectives — competent, mesne, superior. Each has a special meaning for the purposes of Part II of the Act.

Competent landlord

References to the landlord normally refer to the 'competent' landlord, i.e. the person who, at the time, has

(a) An interest in reversion expectant (whether immediately or not) on the termination of the relevant tenancy and
(b) An interest which is either the fee simple or a tenancy which will not come to an end within fourteen months and further that no notice has been given by virtue of which it will come to an end within fourteen months

The competent landlord is the person entitled to give and receive notices and conduct negotiations under Part II.

Mesne landlord

The activities of the competent landlord are binding on all mesne landlords holding interest between those of the competent landlord and his tenant. Where notices are given or

agreements reached without the consent of the mesne landlord or landlords, he or they are entitled to compensation
from the competent landlord for any consequential loss.
Where the competent landlord seeks consent, that consent
shall not be unreasonably withheld although it may be given
subject to reasonable conditions including modification
of the proposed notice or agreement or the payment of
compensation. Questions as to whether consent has been
unreasonably withheld will be determined by the courts.

Superior landlord

Where the competent landlord is not the freeholder and his
interest is a tenancy which will come or can be brought to
an end within sixteen months and he gives the tenant notice
to quit or receives a request from the tenant for a new
tenancy, he is required to send a copy to his immediate
landlord who, if he too is a tenant must send a copy to his
immediate landlord also.

A superior landlord who becomes the competent landlord
within two months of a notice to quit given under section 25
may give notice that he withdraws the notice previously given
in which case it shall cease to have effect. He is not barred
from giving a further notice under the Act.

6.3   TENANCIES EXCLUDED

There are specific exclusions so that the Act does not apply
to —

(a) A tenancy of an agricultural holding
(b) A tenancy created by a mining lease: defined as a lease
    for any mining purpose or purposes, while mining purposes
    include the sinking and searching for, winning, working,
    getting, making merchantable, smelting or otherwise con-
    verting or working for the purpose of any manufacture,
    carrying away and disposing of mines and materials in or
    under land and the erection of buildings and the execution
    of engineering and other works suitable for those pur-
    poses
(c) A tenancy protected by the Rent Acts (or which would
    have been but for the fact that the rent reserved is less
    than two-thirds of the rateable value)

(d) A tenancy of premises licensed for the sale of intoxicating liquor for consumption on the premises except where the premises are ones granted an excise licence at a reduced rate or where the Commissioners of Customs and Excise certify that such a reduction would have been made had an application been made. This exception is intended to apply to premises where the licence is ancillary to the main purpose of the business

(e) A tenancy granted by reason that the tenant was holder of an office, appointment or employment from the grantor which continues only so long as the tenant holds that position. Where the tenancy was created after the commencement of the 1954 Act, the exemption will apply only where the tenancy was granted by an instrument in writing which expressed the purpose for which the tenancy was granted.

(f) A tenancy granted for a term certain not exceeding six months unless the tenancy contains provisions for renewing the term or extending it beyond six months or the tenant and his predecessor in the business have been in occupation for a period exceeding twelve months

6.4 CONTRACTING OUT

The parties to a lease are not in general in a position to enter into any agreement which purports to preclude the tenant from making an application or a request for a new tenancy or provides for the termination or the surrender of the tenancy on making such an application or request or imposes any penalty on the tenant for so doing. Any such agreement will be void although it will not invalidate the remainder of the agreement.

An exception is made so as to enable the landlord and tenant to enter into an agreement for the grant of a future tenancy of the holding or of the holding with other land on terms and from a date specified in the agreement. This exception is necessary to sanction removal of the tenant's right to claim a new tenancy, a right no longer needed once the agreement has been entered into. The current tenancy will then no longer be a tenancy to which Part II applies although it will continue in force until the start of the new tenancy by virtue of these provisions.

Similarly, any agreement purporting to restrict the right to compensation where the tenant or the tenant and his predecessor in the business have occupied the premises for the purposes of a business carried on by the occupier or for those and other purposes during the whole of the five years immediately preceding the date on which the tenant is to quit the holding shall be void. The parties may reach agreement as to the amount of compensation once the right has accrued. Where the above provisions are not satisfied, the right to compensation may be modified or excluded.

These rules were found in practice to preclude lettings where although the tenant recognized the need for the landlord to obtain possession at some specified future date, he was not in a position to enter into an undertaking to give up the premises when required. The 1969 Act therefore introduced a sub-section to enable the parties to make a joint application to the court to authorize an agreement excluding the provisions of sections 24 to 28 of the 1954 Act and, again on a joint application, to authorize an agreement for the surrender of the tenancy on such date or in such circumstances and on such terms, if any, as may be specified.

It has been a common practice where a tenant wishes to assign to require him first to offer to surrender his lease to the landlord: on the landlord's refusal to accept a surrender or his failure to take up the offer, the tenant was free to assign, subject to the landlord's consent but not to be withheld unreasonably. It has now been held that such a provision is void because it precludes the tenant from making an application or request under Part II or provides for the termination or surrender of the tenancy in that event contrary to section 38(1) of the Act (Allnatt London Properties Ltd *v*. Newton 1980).

6.5   CONTINUATION OF TENANCY

It is provided by section 24 that no tenancy to which Part II of the Act applies shall come to an end unless terminated according to the provisions of Part II. Even though the original lease is for a term certain, the tenancy will continue unless the landlord serves notice to terminate the tenancy under section 25 or the tenant makes a request for a new tenancy under section 26.

In either case there is an interim continuation of the tenancy for a period of three months beginning with the date on which the application is determined and finally disposed of by the court: where the landlord's notice to quit or the tenant's request for a new tenancy specified a later date, then that date will prevail.

Where the tenant wishes to apply to the court for a new tenancy he must within two months of the date of the landlord's notice notify the landlord in writing that he is not willing to give up the tenancy. Unless agreement has been reached in the meantime, he must make application to court for a new tenancy not less than two nor more than four months after the landlord's notice or the tenant's request as the case may be.

An application to the court for a new tenancy has the effect of continuing the old tenancy for a period of three months beyond the date on which the application is finally disposed of but the period commences only from the date by which the proceedings on the application have been determined and any time for appealing has expired (section 64(1) and (2)). The effect is to leave a degree of uncertainty as to the expiry of the new lease granted by the court. This problem was overcome in Chipperfield *v.* Shell UK Ltd 1980 and Warwick and Warwick (Philately) Ltd *v.* Shell UK Ltd 1980 by ordering that the new tenancies should end on 31 July 1983.

It is essential that application to the court is made within the statutory period of four months. Stile Hall Properties Ltd *v.* Gooch 1968 concerned a tenant's request which was not followed up in time. The court pointed out that the tenancy came to an end automatically at the date immediately before that specified by the tenant for the commencement of her new tenancy. As she had not commenced proceedings within the time allowed that put an end to the matter.

6.5.1 Interim rent

The landlord may apply to the court to determine an interim rent for the period during which the tenancy continues by virtue of section 24, payment at that rate to be made from the date on which the proceedings were commenced or the date specified in the landlord's notice or the tenant's request, whichever is the later.

The court is required to determine a rent which it would be reasonable for the tenant to pay having regard to the rent payable under the terms of the tenancy but otherwise subject to sub-sections 1 and 2 of section 34 (the statutory disregards in assessing rent under a tenancy granted by order of the court) on the basis of a new tenancy from year to year of the whole of the property comprised in the tenancy.

In Regis Property Co. Ltd *v*. Lewis & Peat Ltd the Court took the view that it should have regard to the existing rent only where it provided some evidence of market value: in later cases this view was supplanted by the interpretation of Meggary J. who suggested that one purpose of the provisions for the assessment of interim rent was to enable a 'cushioning' effect where the market rent was considerably above the existing rent (English Exporters (London) Ltd *v*. Eldonwall Ltd). The courts have developed an approach which makes an allowance for the year to year nature of the hypothetical tenancy and a further allowance to soften the otherwise sharp increase in the rent payable.

The interpretation employed in particular cases ranges from the simple to the detailed. In UDS Tailoring Ltd *v*. B. L. Holdings Ltd where the existing rent was £5250, the new rent was assessed at £21385.60 and reduced by 10% by £19247.04 to reflect the year-to-year basis of the interim rent.

In a recent case, careful calculations by Finlay J. reduced the rent of £12500 assessed for the new tenancy to £9200 for the amount payable as interim rent (Janes (Gowns) Ltd *v*. Harlow Development Corporation). In arriving at the latter figure, he deducted 10% from the original figure of £11372 (which had been increased to £12500 to take account of value increases since the end of the tenancy) to arrive at £10235 and a further 10% to give £9212 (rounded to £9200) to reflect the 'tempering' effect of the statutory provision. (It is of some interest to note that the judge ordered an upwards or downwards rent review provision.)

The doubt that once existed as to the status of an interim rent application following withdrawal of an application for a new tenancy was resolved in Michael Kramer & Co. *v*. Airways Pension Fund. It was held that the interim rent application stands apart and survives withdrawal of the other application.

Where the tenant wishes to withdraw in a case within the jurisdiction of the High Court, he must obtain leave from the Court and the current tenancy will run for three months after leave has been given (Covell Matthews & Partners *v*. French Woods Ltd).

The interim rent should reflect any lack of repair for which the landlord is responsible. The court may fix an interim rent on the assumption that the premises are in a satisfactory state of repair but reduced so long as it takes for the necessary repairs to be completed (Fawke *v*. Viscount Chelsea).

In practice, it is usual to defer application for an interim rent pending the hearing of the landlord's application or the tenant's request so as to avoid the duplication of valuation evidence.

The valuation problems have been considered by the courts. In English Exporters (London) Ltd *v*. Eldonwall Ltd 1973 Megarry J. observed

'I would only add that the process of applying section 34 to a hypothetical yearly tenancy is one that, at least under present conditions, may often have an air of unreality about it and that would puzzle the most expert of valuers'

But valuers are used to valuation constraints: one aspect of valuation concerns the adaptation of evidence derived from one transaction to the circumstances of another.

In Ratners (Jewellers) Ltd *v*. Lemnoll Ltd 1980 both valuers first assessed the market rental value on the basis of a lease with 5 year reviews. The principles laid down in the Eldonwall case were applied with the result that, after hearing the evidence Dillon J. deducted 15% for the difference between a term of years and a yearly tenancy and 5% of the resultant sum for the stringency of the user clause. The arithmetic produced a figure of £19 582 which the judge reduced to £17 500 having regard to the existing rent (a reference to the requirements of section 24A of the 1954 Act and to the direction in subsection (3) that in determining an interim rent, the court shall have regard to the rent payable under the terms of the tenancy.)

The judge remarked that where, as in this case

'...two deductions fall to be made and the resultant figure has then to be tempered by having regard to the rent under the existing lease, mathematical precision in computing each deduction is hardly necessary'

As noted above, once a new agreement is entered into the current tenancy is continued until the commencement of the new agreement by section 24 but is no longer subject to the provisions of Part II of the Act.

Section 24 does not affect a tenancy terminated by the tenant either by notice to quit or surrender or by forfeiture, though relief may be obtained from the court where the forfeiture is of a superior tenancy. In an endeavour to prevent avoidance or abuse of these provisions, there are restrictions on the issue of a notice to quit before the tenant had been in occupation under the tenancy for one month or, in the case of a surrender, the instrument was executed before, or was executed in pursuance of an agreement made before, the tenant had been in occupation under the tenancy for one month.

6.6   TERMINATION OF TENANCY

Apart from a tenant's request for a new tenancy, a tenancy may be terminated by

(a) A notice to quit by the tenant
(b) A notice to quit served by the landlord
(c) Surrender or forfeiture

Where notice is served by the tenant, it must be of the proper length as required by the agreement. Where the tenancy is for a certain term, the tenant must serve notice not later than three months from the end of the term, otherwise the tenancy will continue in accordance with section 24.

The Act provides that notices should be sent by registered post while the *Recorded Delivery Service Act 1962* modifies the requirement to enable such notices to be sent by the recorded delivery service. Where a notice was sent by ordinary post, it was held that the tenant must prove service within the statutory period if he was not to lose his rights (Chiswell *v*. Griffon Land and Estates Ltd 1975).

The Act is concerned mainly with the notice served by the landlord under section 25. There is a prescribed form which gives the tenant notice of his rights and informs him whether the landlord is prepared to grant a new lease and if not, the reasons for wishing to obtain possession. A notice not in substantially the form prescribed would probably be bad, though the courts have upheld notices where the content of the notes forming part of the prescribed notice was inaccurate in that no alterations had been made to take account of amendments introduced by the 1969 Act.

In Tegerdine *v*. Brooks 1977 surveyors served a notice to quit which was incomplete in that three of the notes were omitted as being irrelevant in the particular circumstances. The notice was held to be substantially to the same effect as the statutory form. In the course of the judgment, attention was drawn to a statement of the law made in Bolton's (House Furnishers) Ltd *v*. Oppenheim 1959

'It is clear, I think ... that this notice should be construed liberally and provided that it does give the real substance of the information required, then the mere omission of certain details, or the failure to embody in the notice the full provisions of the section of the Act referred to will not in fact invalidate the notice'

According to the test laid down in Carradine Properties Ltd *v*. Aslam 1976 and adopted in Germax Securities Ltd *v*. Spiegal 1979 the questions to be put are 'Is the notice quite clear to a reasonable tenant reading it?' and 'Is it plain that he cannot be misled by it?'

The matter has been considered once again in Philipson-Stow *v*. Trevor Square Ltd. After a review of the authorities, Goulding J. concluded that a notice which, though inaccurately expressed was not deceptive or misleading and which made clear which of the seven grounds the landlord was relying on, was valid.

As a first step, the tenant must notify the landlord in writing, within two months of the giving of the notice, whether or not, at the date of termination, he will be willing to give up possession. Secondly, if he wishes to obtain an order for the grant of a new tenancy, he must apply to the court not less than two or more than four months after the landlord has given notice. Failure to respect the time-table laid down will preclude any further action on the part of the tenant.

Where the court is closed by authority on the final day of the period of notice, it has been held that the tenant is entitled to give notice on the next working day — in this case the day after Easter Monday (Hodgson *v*. Armstrong and Another 1966).

There are prescribed forms for the various notices: the two most common are reproduced in the Appendix.

6.7   GROUNDS FOR OPPOSITION TO NEW TENANCY

Notice to quit is often served simply as a necessary preliminary to renegotiating the terms of the lease and in particular the rent payable thereunder. The landlord is required to state as part of the notice whether he would oppose an application to the court for the grant of a new tenancy. Nevertheless the tenant must serve notice within the period laid down to protect his rights should agreement prove impossible and he wishes to claim a new tenancy. Where the tenant is willing to give up possession he need take no action and will vacate in accordance with the notice.

Where the landlord wishes to obtain possession, he must state in the notice that he would oppose an application to the court for the grant of a new tenancy, stating the gound on which he relies. Section 30 of the Act sets out the grounds on which the landlord may oppose an application.

6.7.1   Ground (a) — state of repair

Where under the current tenancy the tenant has any

obligations as respects the repair and maintenance of the holding, that the tenant ought not to be granted a new tenancy in view of the state of repair of the holding, being a state resulting from the tenant's failure to comply with the said obligations

The court has discretion, the exercise of which will be influenced, no doubt, by the severity of the breach. In Lyons *v*. Central Commercial Properties Ltd 1958 it was held that serious breaches had occurred and not been remedied and that relief ought not to be granted. The tenant's negotiations to transfer his interest to a third party were not relevant to the court's determination.

6.7.2   Ground (b) — persistent delay in paying rent

That the tenant ought not to be granted a new tenancy in view of his persistent delay in paying rent which has become due

There must be not only delay but persistent delay: the implication is that the delay must occur on more than one isolated occasion: the precise interpretation is left to the discretion of the court. The frequency and length of delay are relevant as are the additional management costs incurred by the landlord as a result of the delay (Hopcutt *v*. Carver 1969).

6.7.3   Ground (c) — other substantial breaches

That the tenant ought not to be granted a new tenancy in view of other substantial breaches by him of his obligations under the current tenancy, or for any other reason connected with the tenant's use or management of the holding

Whether a breach is substantial is a matter of fact on the particular circumstances including any waiver by the landlord (but see Norton *v*. Charles Deane Productions Ltd 1970: a breach of covenant may be insufficient as a cause for obtaining forfeiture of a lease but may be adequate for refusing renewal of a tenancy).

The court is entitled to consider the whole of the tenant's conduct in relation to his obligations under the tenancy and need not limit itself to the grounds stated in the landlord's notice (Eichner *v*. Midland Bank Executor and Trustee Co. Ltd 1970).

The court has a discretion which was considered by Ormerod L. J. in Lyons *v*. Central Commercial Properties Ltd 1958

> 'without attempting to define the precise limits of that discretion the judge, as I see it, may have regard to the conduct of the tenant in relation to his obligation'

The reference in this ground to the tenant's use or management of the holding is a useful additional provision.

In a case where a tenant was using premises in breach of an enforcement notice and where he intended to continue doing so if granted a new tenancy, it was held that the court could not condone the tenant's illegal conduct by making an order for a new tenancy which would create an illegal contract (Turner and Bell *v*. Searles (Stanford-le-Hope) Ltd 1977).

6.7.4   Ground (d) — provision of alternative accommodation

> That the landlord has offered and is willing to provide or secure the provision of alternative accommodation for the tenant, that the terms on which the alternative accommodation is available are reasonable having regard to the terms of the current tenancy and to all other relevant circumstances and that the accommodation and the time at which it will be available are suitable for the tenant's requirements (including the requirement to preserve goodwill) having regard to the nature and class of his business and to the situation and extent of, and facilities afforded by, the holding

It may be that the offer on reasonable terms of part only of the premises presently occupied would be regarded in certain circumstances as suitable alternative accommodation.

The ground is otherwise unlikely to be much used except where the landlord wishes to redevelop or occupy the premises and is able to offer suitable premises nearby.

6.7.5   Ground (e) — uneconomic letting of part

Where the current tenancy was created by the sub-letting of part only of the property comprised in a superior tenancy and the landlord is the owner of an interest in reversion expectant on the termination of that superior tenancy, that the aggregate of the rents reasonably obtainable on separate lettings of the holding and the remainder of that property would be substantially less than the rent reasonably obtainable on a letting of that property as a whole, that on the termination of the current tenancy the landlord requires possession of the holding for the purpose of letting or otherwise disposing of the said property as a whole, and that in view thereof the tenant ought not to be granted a new tenancy

This is essentially a financial or economic ground. The landlord needs to show that his return would be substantially improved by letting or disposing of the property as a whole. Not a ground much used.

In Greaves Organisation Ltd *v*. Stanhope Gate Property Co. Ltd 1973 the landlords' claim for possession failed because they were unable to establish that the aggregate of the rents would be *substantially* less than if let as a whole.

6.7.6   Ground (f) — intention to demolish or reconstruct

That on the termination of the current tenancy the landlord intends to demolish or reconstruct the premises comprised in the holding or a substantial part of those premises or to carry out substantial work of construction on the holding or part thereof and that he could not reasonably do so without obtaining possession of the holding

The effect of this ground is altered substantially by the provisions of a new section 31A introduced by the *Law of Property Act 1969* which provides, in part

'31A-(1) Where the landlord opposes an application under s 24(1) of this Act on the ground specified in para (f) of s 30(1) of this Act the court shall not hold that the landlord could not reasonably carry out the demolition, reconstruction or work of construction intended without obtaining possession of the holding if —

(a) the tenant agrees to the inclusion in the terms of the new tenancy of terms giving the landlord access and other facilities for carrying out the work intended and, given that access and those facilities, the landlord could reasonably carry out the work without obtaining possession of the holding and without interfering to a substantial extent or for a substantial time with the use of the holding for the purposes of the business carried on by the tenant: or

(b) the tenant is willing to accept a tenancy of an economically separable part of the holding and either para (a) of this section is satisfied with respect to that part or possession of the remainder of the holding would be reasonably sufficient to enable the landlord to carry out the intended work.'

The section provides in sub-section (2) a definition of 'economically separable part', no doubt thereby avoiding much discussion and argument as to what is and what is not to be regarded as separable under this section:

'(2) For the purposes of subs (1)(b) of this section a part of a holding shall be deemed to be an economically separable part if, and only if, the aggregate of the rents which, after the completion of the intended work, would be reasonably obtainable on separate lettings of that part and the remainder of the premises affected by or resulting from the work would not be substantially less than the rent which would then be reasonably obtainable on a letting of those premises as a whole'

'Intention' (in relation to the landlord's intention to demolish or reconstruct) was defined by Asquith L. J. as the need for the proposal to have

'moved out of the zone of contemplation — out of the sphere of the tentative, the provisional and the exploratory — into the valley of decision'

Intention must be established as at the date of the hearing of the application (Betty's Cafes Ltd *v*. Phillips Furnishing Stores Ltd 1958).

The more firm the landlord's proposal, the better the chance of proving an intention. Architect's plans, estimates, planning permission will all be persuasive although the main question is not whether the landlord has permission but rather the prospects of obtaining permission (Gregson *v*. Cyril Lord 1962). The test there was said to be whether a reasonable man would believe, on the evidence, that there was a reasonable prospect of getting that permission or consent.

Intention should be firmly evidenced: for example in the case of a company by a board minute.

In H. L. Bolton Engineering Co. Ltd *v*. T. J. Graham and Sons Ltd 1957 it was held that the intention of three directors was the intention of the company, even though there had been no board meeting. A similar conclusion was reached relating to the intention of a local authority (Poppett's (Caterers) Ltd *v*. Maidenhead Borough Council 1971) but it is clearly safer to have a formal resolution.

Reconstruction envisages substantial structural work (Joel *v* Swaddle 1957 where a proposal to convert two single shop units to form part of an amusement arcade was held to be reconstruction) or rebuilding (Percy E. Cadle and Co. Ltd *v*. Jacmarch Properties Ltd 1957 where a proposal to combine into a self-contained unit three floors previously held separately was considered not to be reconstruction). The ground failed in Heath *v*. Drown 1972 where the landlord had power by virtue of the current tenancy agreement to enter under a repair clause and carry out necessary work.

An unusual case is noted here. A tenant company applied to the County Court for the outstanding terms of a new lease to be determined: the judge ordered a five year lease with a break at three years based entirely on detailed evidence of the intention of the plaintiff company to re-develop the premises — yet earlier the landlords had not opposed the grant of a new tenancy or called in aid section 30(1)(f). The Court of Appeal dismissed the tenant company's appeal in what must be regarded as an unsatisfactory case on the facts disclosed (Amika Motors Ltd *v*. Colebrook Holdings Ltd).

The courts are not prepared to countenance an application which seeks to 'play the system' to gain further delays (A. J. A. Smith Transport Ltd *v*. British Railways Board).

6.7.7   Ground (g) — landlord's intention to occupy

Subject as hereinafter provided, that on the termination of the current tenancy the landlord intends to occupy the holding for the purposes, or partly for the purposes, of a business to be carried on by him therein, or as his residence

There is an important limiting proviso to the effect that the landlord shall not be entitled to oppose an application on this ground if the interest of the landlord was purchased or created after the beginning of the period of five years and ending with the termination of the current tenancy where at all times the tenancy has been one subject to Part II of the Act.

The landlord must have a firm intention to occupy and evidence of his proposals for alterations would be helpful in support of his intentions under this ground.

The intention to occupy must be more than a device to obtain possession and sell after occupying for a short time (Willis *v*. Association of Universities of the British Commonwealth 1965) and would be strengthened by an undertaking to the court on the part of the landlord to occupy in the event of obtaining possession (Espresso Coffee Machine Co. Ltd *v*. Guardian Assurance Co. Ltd 1959).

In Method Developments Ltd *v* Jones 1971 the landlords succeeded under this ground even though they did not intend to occupy the whole of the premises immediately and would leave a part unused. But where it was proposed to obtain possession of a collection of buildings and a yard and to incorporate the cleared land with other land in order to build a filling station on the combined site, the landlords did not succeed in their claim (Nursey *v*. P. Currie (Dartford) Ltd 1959).

In a more recent case, the landlord sought to obtain possession to enable him to erect a building on what was then a car park operated by the tenant in conjunction with his business on adjoining land. The court distinguished Nursey on the grounds that the landlord merely intended to place a building on the site and not to create a wider scheme and dismissed the tenant's appeal (Cam Gears Ltd *v*. Cunningham 1981).

The landlord may occupy by a manager or an agent (Cafeteria (Keighley) Ltd *v*. Harrison 1956).

Under certain conditions, the landlord may obtain possession to enable a company which he controls to occupy the premises (see section 6.10.1).

6.8   ORDER FOR GRANT OF NEW TENANCY

If the tenant is able to surmount the obstacles placed in his way by the reasons given for termination of a tenancy in a landlord's notice to quit or in reply to his request for a new tenancy, he is entitled to an order of the court for the grant of a tenancy for a term not exceeding fourteen years.

The court may, if it thinks fit, include a provision for varying the rent during the term of the new tenancy. Where the current tenancy includes rights enjoyed by the tenant in connection with the holding, such rights are to be included except as otherwise agreed or in default of agreement, determined by the court. This provision enables the landlord to make a case for the exclusion of rights previously enjoyed in connection with the holding under the current tenancy and removes the mandatory nature of the original subsection (3) of section 32. Where the tenant is willing to accept a tenancy of part of the holding, the order made by the court shall be an order for the grant of a new tenancy of that part only.

Where the court makes an order, the terms of the tenancy shall be such as may be agreed between the landlord and the tenant or, in default of agreement, determined by the court. The court is required to have regard to the terms of the current tenancy and to all relevant circumstances. The majority of disputes are confined to the rent payable, although there is often disagreement about the term to be granted, the frequency of rent reviews and the other terms to be included. Clearly, the terms agreed between the parties or fixed by the court will affect the rental value which should not therefore be determined until all the other terms are known.

Trading accounts are admissible in evidence as to what a new tenant, an outsider, would pay although the accounts should not be used for the purpose of assessing what the present tenant could pay (Harewood Hotels Ltd *v.* Harris 1957).

An important principle was established in O'May and others *v.* City of London Real Property Co. Ltd 1979. The defendant landlord proposed to amend the terms of an earlier lease on granting a new term of three years, so as to make the tenant liable for maintenance of the building and equipment and for depreciation of plant and equipment and suggested a reduction of the rent of 50 pence per square foot per annum to take account of this shift of burden. The attraction from the landlord company's point of view was that it would then have had a 'clear lease' which on the evidence would increase the capital value by between one and two million pounds by removing the speculative element in fluctuating costs for which the landlord was responsible. The valuers for landlord and tenant were able to agree that the reduction of 50 pence represented the additional liability cast on the tenants. Shaw L. J. opined that the landlord's revised terms introduced a radical change in the balance of rights and responsibilities, of advantage and detriment, of security and risk. Brightman L. J. agreed that this case had to be considered under section 35 and not section 34 because the substantial issue was not the amount or calculation of the rent but the incidence of certain unusual financial burdens which would have the effect of controlling the rent. He went on to remark that a short term tenant is not adequately compensated by a small reduction in rent for his assumption of the financial risks implicit in the maintenance of the structure of an office block. Those risks should properly be borne by the owner of the inheritance: such risks are indeterminate in amount and could prove to be wholly out of proportion to the very limited interest held by a short term tenant. Buckley L. J. thought that the new tenancy should, *mutatis mutandis*, be on similar terms to the existing tenancy. Any departure from those terms would require explanation, that is to say justification (Cardshops Ltd *v.*

Davies 1971 where four tests were propounded by Goulding J. and adopted in the O'May case although there they led to an opposite conclusion). The reduction in the rental which was said to compensate the tenants for assuming those risks was far from being an indemnity against them. The tenants might find themselves saddled with very heavy capital expenditure for which the reduction in rent would by no means compensate them, except possibly in the very long run . . . which would be no comfort to a tenant for a relatively short period.

The four tests laid down by Goulding J. were:

1. Has the party seeking an alteration in the terms given a reason?
2. Is the adjustment of rent proposed adequate to compensate the party opposing the alteration?
3. Will the proposal adversely affect the security of the tenants?
4. If the answer to the first two questions is 'Yes' and to the third 'No', does the proposed alteration appear to be fair and reasonable as between the parties?

A restriction on the use to which premises may be put may result in the determination of a reduced rent. In Charles Clements (London) Ltd *v*. Rank City Wall Ltd 1978 the landlords sought to relax the covenant restricting use of the premises to the business of a retail cutler by adding to the expression 'without the landlord's consent in writing' a rider 'such consent not to be unreasonably withheld'. The tenants objected to the relaxation which would have had the effect of increasing the rental value. The tenants' objection was upheld.

Where the rent is determined by the court it is to be the rent at which the holding might reasonably be expected to be let in the open market by a willing lessor, disregarding —

(a) Any effect on rent of the fact that the tenant or his predecessors in title have been in occupation of the holding
(b) Any goodwill attached to the holding by reason of the carrying on thereat of the business of the tenant (whether by him or by a predecessor of his in that business
(c) Any effect on rent of an improvement carried out by a

person who at that time was the tenant but only if it was carried out otherwise than in pursuance of an obligation to his immediate landlord and either it was carried out during the current tenancy or the following conditions are satisfied —

   (i) That it was completed not more than 21 years before the application for a new tenancy was made and

   (ii) That the holding or any part of it affected by the improvement has at all times since the completion of the improvement been comprised in tenancies which include premises which are occupied by the tenant and are so occupied for the purposes of a business carried on by him or for those and other purposes and

   (iii) That at the termination of each of those tenancies the tenant did not quit

(d) In the case of a holding comprising licensed premises, any addition to its value attributable to the licence where it appears to the court that the benefit of the licence belongs to the tenant

6.9　COMPENSATION ON TERMINATION OF TENANCY

On leaving the premises the tenant may be entitled to compensation for disturbance and also for any improvements carried out by him. He may also be able to claim compensation when subsequent events show that the court was induced to refuse an order for the grant of a new tenancy by misrepresentation or the concealment of material facts.

6.9.1　Compensation for disturbance

Where the only grounds specified in the landlord's notice related to one or more of those contained in (e) (f) and (g) above, the tenant is entitled to compensation. Grounds (a) (b) (c) and (d) do not attract compensation. Where more than one ground is stated and one of those grounds is from the latter group, the tenant's entitlement to compensation will turn on whether the court finds that it is precluded from making an order by reason only of the grounds set out in (e) to (g).

The amount of compensation payable to the tenant is

based on the rateable value of the premises. A payment of four and one half times the rateable value is payable where during the whole of the fourteen years immediately preceding the termination of the current tenancy the premises have been occupied for the purposes of a business carried on by the occupier or for those and other purposes or, where the present occupier has not been in occupation for the whole of the fourteen years, if he is the successor to the business carried on by the person who was the occupier immediately before him.

Where compensation is payable but these conditions cannot be satisfied, the amount will be a sum two and one quarter times the rateable value. (*The Landlord and Tenant Act 1954* (*Appropriate Multiplier*) *Regulations 1981* (SI 1981/69))

Until 1969, the tenant's application to court was a prerequisite of his entitlement to compensation. As a result of amendments introduced at that time, he is now entitled to compensation under grounds (e) (f) and (g) where no application is made or, having been made, is withdrawn. Should the tenant wish to resist other grounds not entitling him to compensation he must still apply to the court.

6.9.2 Compensation for misrepresentation

Where the court refuses an order for the grant of a new tenancy and it is subsequently shown that the court was induced to refuse the order by misrepresentation or by the concealment of material facts, the court may order the landlord to pay a sufficient sum as compensation for damage or loss sustained by the tenant.

There is no formula and no limit: the provision was undoubtedly intended to discourage irresponsible action by enabling the possibility of substantial damages being awarded. The provision makes it clear that the landlord involved in the application is responsible for payment and the tenant is eligible to make the claim: the burden and benefits do not pass to subsequent parties.

6.9.3 Compensation for improvements

The *Landlord and Tenant Act 1927* survives, subject to certain amendments made by Part III of the 1954 Act, to enable the tenant to claim compensation for improvements in certain circumstances. Certain differences of treatment apply where the contract was made before 10 December 1953: only the provisions relating to contracts entered into on or after the date are discussed here.

Where a tenant proposes to make an improvement he is required to serve on his landlord notice of his intention together with a specification and plan showing the proposed improvement and the part of the existing premises affected. The landlord may object to the proposals within three months after service of the notice whereupon the tenant may apply to the court for a certificate that the improvement is a proper improvement and the court must be satisfied that the improvement will add to the letting value of the premises at the termination of the tenancy. It must also be satisfied that the improvement is reasonable and suitable in character and will not diminish the value of any other property belonging to the same landlord or to any superior landlord from whom the immediate landlord holds directly or indirectly.

The court is empowered to make such modifications as it thinks fit or to impose such other conditions as it may think reasonable.

The court shall not issue a certificate where the landlord shows that he has offered to carry out the work himself in consideration of a reasonable increase in rent or of such rent as the court may determine, unless it is shown subsequently that the landlord has failed to carry out the work.

The tenant is not entitled to claim compensation unless he has served notice of the proposal and obtained the agreement of his landlord or, in default thereof, of the court. The tenant may require the landlord to furnish him with a certificate to the effect that the improvement has been duly executed on payment by the tenant of any reasonable costs incurred by the landlord: where the landlord refuses or fails within one month after the tenant's request to furnish a certificate, the tenant may apply to the court. Possession of a certificate may avoid argument at a later stage when the tenant seeks to make a claim for compensation.

Where the tenant carries out improvements after 1 October 1954 under a statutory obligation he may make a claim for compensation at the end of his tenancy: approval of the landlord is of course inappropriate although he must be given proper notice and the tenant may obtain at his own expense a certificate of execution. It is not clear whether the landlord may offer to carry out the work himself.

Work carried out by the tenant in pursuance of a contractual obligation is outside the scope of the Act and does not qualify for compensation.

Having laid a proper basis for compensation for improvements, the tenant must observe the various time limits laid down for making a valid claim on quitting the premises. Where the tenancy expires by effluxion of time the tenant must serve notice not earlier than six nor later than three months before the end of the tenancy.

A claim where the tenancy is terminated by a notice to quit given by the landlord or the tenant must be made within three months from the date on which notice is given. Where the tenancy is terminated by a tenant's request for a new tenancy any claim must be made within three months from the date on which the landlord opposed the request or, where the request is not opposed, within three months from the latest date on which he could have opposed it. Where a tenancy is terminated by forfeiture or re-entry, the claim must be made within three months from the effective date of the court order for possession. Where the tenancy is terminated by re-entry without a court order, a similar time limit runs from the date of re-entry.

The amount of compensation for improvements may not exceed

(a) The net addition to the value of the holding as a whole which may be determined to be the direct result of the improvement or
(b) The reasonable cost of carrying out the improvement at the termination of the tenancy, subject to deduction of an amount equal to the cost (if any) of putting the works into a reasonable state of repair, except where such cost is part of the tenant's liability under his lease

Any proposals by the landlord to demolish or alter the premises or to change their use are likely to have an adverse effect on the tenant's claim. Where compensation has been reduced or refused by the court following evidence of such proposals, the court may authorize a further application for compensation where effect is not given to the intention within a time fixed by the court.

6.10   MISCELLANEOUS MATTERS

The 1954 Act created unexpected problems for a landlord wishing to obtain possession for occupation by a business carried on by a company which he controls and for tenants in partnership. The 1969 Act introduced amendments designed to overcome the problems.

6.10.1   Companies

The new provision (section 30(3)) enables the landlord to oppose a request for the grant of a new tenancy of premises on the ground that the company in which he has a controlling interest intends to occupy the premises for the purpose of its business.

For this purpose he has a controlling interest if either he is a member of the company and able to appoint or remove the directors or the majority of them or he holds more than one-half of the company's equity share capital in his own right.

6.10.2   Partnerships

A case before the Court of Appeal in 1968 brought to light a problem where one of the joint tenants does not join in a tenant's request for a new tenancy. It was held that an application from one tenant was not valid since he was not the tenant for the purposes of section 24(1).

As a result, a new section (41A) was introduced to deal with the situation where a tenancy of business premises is held jointly by two or more persons all of whom at some time during the existence of the tenancy carried on a business (not necessarily the same business) but, which is now carried on by one or some only of the joint tenant or tenants, the remaining tenant or tenants having no business occupation of any part of the property.

The remaining business tenant or tenants are enabled

to serve a valid tenant's request for a new tenancy (under section 26) or a notice to quit (under section 27) provided that it sets out the facts of the changed circumstances. The business tenant will be able to obtain a new tenancy either alone or jointly with other partners while the court may require guarantors or sureties as a condition of a new tenancy where appropriate. The business tenants will also be able to obtain statutory compensation and to exercise all other rights under the Act.

6.10.3 Notices under the Landlord and Tenant Act 1954

Prescribed notices under the *Landlord and Tenant Act 1954* have been revised by *Landlord and Tenant Act 1954*, Part II (Notices) Regulations 1983 (SI No. 133).

Two of those in most common use, the Landlord's Notice to Terminate Business Tenancy and the Tenant's Request for New Tenancy of Business Premises, are reproduced complete with notes in the Appendix.

FURTHER READING

Aldridge, T. M. (1978) *Letting Business Premises*, Oyez Publishing, London.

Fox-Andrews, J. (1978) *Business Tenancies*, 3rd edn, Estates Gazette, London.

Wellings, V. G. (1978) *Woodfall's Landlord and Tenant*, Sweet and Maxwell, London.

CHAPTER 7

Business tenancies: rent reviews

7.1 INTRODUCTION

Provision for a review of the rent payable during the currency of a lease is now a common feature of leases. This is a development of the last twenty or so years which recognizes the eroding effect of inflation on purchasing power and the need to protect future payments from its worst effects.

Occupation leases for a long term — typically 15, 21 or 25 years — have advantages for both landlord and tenant but each party recognized the need for a regular re-appraisal of the rent paid. The parties' advisers therefore began to incorporate rent review clauses in leases but without always achieving the intended effect. The recent level of litigation is testimony both to the loose drafting of many review clauses and to the continuing ravages of inflation.

It has been common for the landlord to insist on 'upward only' reviews which are hardly reasonable taking account of the uncertainty of the future and which may involve the tenant in onerous financial obligations. Continuing trading problems being experienced by business firms may prepare the ground for a more general acceptance of upward or downward rent reviews: it is interesting to note that the Law Society/RICS precedent printed on pages 104—109 makes provision for such an arrangement.

The parties are required to agree the new rent payable in accordance with the provisions of the particular rent review clause and may be assisted in their interpretation of the effect of the covenant by a number of recent judgments.

The valuer may undertake rental valuations as agent of either landlord or tenant, or in third party proceedings as expert witness, arbitrator or independent surveyor.

7.2   FORMS OF REVIEW CLAUSE

There is a wide variety of review clauses in use and, except where a review is included as one of the terms in any new lease granted by order of the court, the parties are free to agree whatever form appears appropriate. In practice, three basic forms have emerged. Many leases, particularly earlier ones, use as a basis the provisions of section 34 of the *Law of Property Act 1954*. These rather theoretical provisions were designed to guide the courts on tenancy renewals and are not entirely appropriate to the subject of reviews: not surprisingly, the rents resulting have often disappointed one or other of the parties when the precise meaning has been tested before the courts.

Leases granted by landlords experienced in property matters have not always avoided all the pitfalls, but in general have provided clearer and more specific directions for ascertaining the review rent. Indeed, there has been a tendency for long and elaborate clauses setting up a fictitious background against which the rent is to be adjudged.

Finally, the Royal Institution of Chartered Surveyors has co-operated with the Law Society to produce a model rent review clause with alternatives to suit particular circumstances. If adopted on a large scale, many of the current problems would disappear eventually, although given the lifespan of many leases, it is to be expected that unsatisfactorily drafted review clauses will continue to present problems of interpretation for some time to come.

The following pages show a typical 'section 34' type review clause, an independently drafted review clause and a reprint of the model clause referred to above.

7.2.1   A 'section 34' type clause:

'Provided Always and it is hereby agreed that at the expiration of the seventh and fourteenth years of the term hereby granted (the time in each case being computed from the date of the commencement of the said term and being hereinafter referred to as "the date of review") the rent shall from and after the date of review

be such sum as shall be agreed between the Landlords
and the Tenants as representing the fair rack rental market
value of the demised premises for the then residue of the
term of years hereby granted as between a willing landlord
and a willing tenant with vacant possession and in all
respects on the terms and conditions of this Lease (other
than the rent) and if the Landlords and the Tenant shall
be unable to agree on the amount of such rent as aforesaid
the same shall be decided by some competent person to
be agreed to by the Landlords and the Tenants or in the
event of failure so to agree by a person (hereinafter called
"the Arbitrator") to be named by the President for the
time being of the Royal Institution of Chartered Surveyors
who shall act as an arbitrator PROVIDED ALWAYS that
the Landlords and the Tenants and such Arbitrator shall in
agreeing or deciding the amount of the rent upon any such
review disregard:

(a) any effect on the rental value of the demised premises
    of the fact that the Tenants have or their predecessors
    in title have been in occupation of the said premises.
(b) any goodwill attached to the said premises by reason
    of the carrying on thereon of the Tenants' business.
(c) any effect on the rental value of any improvement
    carried out by the Tenants or their predecessors in title
    otherwise than in pursuance of an obligation contained
    in this Lease and in particular but without prejudice to
    the generality of the foregoing any such effect of any
    works of fitting out and finishing the demised premises
    to acceptable office standards carried out by the
    Tenants at the commencement of the term hereby
    created.'

7.2.2   An alternative form of review clause:

PROVIDED ALWAYS THAT AND IT IS HEREBY AGREED
as follows:

(1) The Lessor shall be entitled by notice in writing given to
    the Lessee during the first six months of every fifth year of

the said term to call for a review (at the expense of the lessee) of the yearly rent payable under this Lease and if upon any such review it shall be found that the revised yearly rent (as hereinafter defined) of the demised premises as at the end of such year in which such notice shall have been served shall be greater than the said yearly rent then currently payable following the last previous rent review by virtue of this Clause then as from the end of every such fifth year the yearly rent payable under this Lease shall be increased to the amount of such revised yearly rent as aforesaid.

(2) For the purposes of such respective rent reviews the expression 'the revised yearly rent' means the yearly rent at which the demised premises might reasonably be expected then to be let for use within the meaning of Class III of the Town and Country Planning (Use Classes) Order 1972 in the open market without any premium or fine with vacant possession for a term of five years from the date from which such revised yearly rent is (if at all) to become payable or the residue of the said term then unexpired (whichever be longer) and upon the same terms (save as to rent) as this present lease but disregarding:

   (i) any effect on rent of the occupation by the lessee of the demised premises or of any goodwill attaching to the demised premises by reason only of the lessee having carried on business thereat and

   (ii) any effect on rent of any improvement to the demised premises carried out by the lessee during the currency of the said term otherwise than in pursuance of an obligation arising under this Lease.

(3) Each such rent review shall in the first instance be made by the Lessor and the Lessee or their respective surveyors in collaboration but if no agreement as to the amount of the increase (if any) to be made in the said yearly rent shall have been reached between the parties within two months after the date of the Lessor's notice calling for such review then the question whether the said yearly

rent shall be increased and if so what the amount of the increased yearly rent is to be shall be referred to the decision of a surveyor to be appointed in default of agreement between the parties by the President for the time being of the Royal Institution of Chartered Surveyors and such Surveyor shall in arriving at his decision act as an expert and not an arbitrator (and accordingly the provisions of the Arbitration Act 1950 or any Act or Order for the time being replacing the same shall not apply) and the decision of such Surveyor shall be final and binding on both parties.

(4) If upon any such reviews it shall be agreed or decided that the said yearly rent payable under this Lease is to be increased then the Lessor and the Lessee shall if required forthwith at the expense of the Lessee enter into a Deed supplemental to this Lease specifying and confirming the increased yearly rent to be payable.

(5) If at the end of any rent period the amount of the increased yearly rent for the next rent period shall not then have been agreed or decided in manner aforesaid then in respect of any part of the next rent period falling before such agreement or decision shall have been made the Lessee shall pay rent at such rate at such times and in such manner as shall have been applicable in respect of the last year of the then immediately preceding rent period and any rent in excess of such rent which may be found to be payable hereunder shall be paid (without any deduction) within fourteen days of the date on which the amount of the said increased yearly rent shall have been ascertained.

7.2.3 The RICS – Law Society model clause (reproduced by permission)

...yielding and paying to the landlord yearly rents ascertained in accordance with the next four clauses hereof without any deduction by equal quarterly payments in advance on the usual quarterdays the first payment (being an apportioned sum) to be made on the date hereof

Clause 1.

Definitions

In this deed "review date" means the   day of   in the year 19   and in every   year thereafter and "review period" means the period starting with any review date up to the next review date or starting with the last review date up to the end of the term hereof

Clause 2.

Provisions for revision of rent (see Note 1)

The yearly rent shall be:
(A) until the first review date the rent of £   and
(B) during each successive review period *a rent equal to the rent previously payable hereunder or* such revised rent as may be ascertain as herein provided *whichever be the greater* and

Additional sub-clause for upwards/downwards reviews only

(C) in the event of a revised rent not being ascertain as herein provided the rent payable for the relevant review period shall be the rent payable immediately prior to the commencement of such period

Clause 3.

Ascertainment of amount at landlord's option by arbitrator or independent valuer (see Notes 2 and 3)

Such revised rent for any review period may be agreed at any time between the landlord and the tenant or (in the absence of agreement determined not earlier than the relevant review date at the option of the landlord either by

NOTE 1.

If the reviews are to be "upwards/down-wards" the word in italics should be omitted and paragraph (C) should be added.

NOTE 2.

Only one of the three commencing paragraphs give for Clause 3 should be used. The essential differences are that the

104

Clause 3.

Ascertainment of amount by arbitrator
(see Notes 2 and 3)

an arbitrator or by an independent valuer (acting as an expert and not as an arbitrator) such arbitrator or valuer to be nominated in the absence of agreement by or on behalf of the president for the time being of the Royal Institution of Chartered Surveyors on the application of the landlord made not earlier than six months before the relevant review date *but not later than the end of the relevant review period* and so that in the case of such arbitration or valuation the revised rent to be awarded or determined by the arbitrator or valuer shall be such as he shall decide should be the yearly rent at the relevant review date for the demised premises

—OR—

Such revised rent for any review period may be agreed at any time between the landlord and the tenant or (in the absence of agreement) determined not earlier than the relevant review date by an arbitrator such arbitrator to be nominated in the absence of agreement by or on behalf of the president for the time being of the Royal Institution of Chartered Surveyors on the application of the landlord or the tenant made not earlier than six months before the relevant review date *but not later than the end of the relevant review period* and so that in the case of such arbitration the revised rent to be awarded by the arbitrator shall be such as he shall decide should be the yearly rent at the relevant review date for the demised premises

—OR—

first gives the landlord alone the right to opt for arbitration or independent valuation. The second and third provide respectively for arbitration only and for independent valuation only but both allow either the landlord or the tenant to initiate the process. If the words in italics are included in the commencing paragraph there will be a time limit after which a review can no longer be initiated.

105

Clause 3.

Ascertainment of amount
by independent valuer
(see Notes 2 and 3)

Such revised rent for any review period may be agreed at any time between the landlord and the tenant or (in the absence of agreement) determined not earlier than the relevant review date by an independent valuer (acting as an expert and not as an arbitrator) such valuer to be nominated in the absence of agreement by or on behalf of the president for the time being of the Royal Institution of Chartered Surveyors on the application of the landlord or the tenant made not earlier than six months before the relevant review date *but not later than the end of the relevant review period* and so that in the case of such valuation the revised rent to be determined by the valuer shall be such as he shall decide should be the yearly rent at the relevant review date for the demised premises

Provisions applicable
in all versions of
clause 3

(A) On the following assumptions at that date:

(i) that the demised premises are fit for immediate occupation and use and that no work has been carried out thereon by the tenant its sub-tenants or their predecessors in title during the said term which has diminished the rental value of the demised premises and that in case the demised premises have been destroyed or damaged they have been fully restored

(ii) that the demised premises are available to let by a willing landlord to a willing tenant as a whole without a premium but with vacant possession and subject to the provisions of this lease (other than the amount of the rent hereby reserved but including the provisions for rent review) for a term equal to the original term of this lease

(iii) that the covenants herein contained on the part of the tenant have been fully performed and observed

AND having regard to open market rental values current at the relevant review date

(B) But disregarding:

(i) any effect on rent of the fact that the tenant its sub-tenants or their respective predecessors in title have been in occupation of the demised premises

(ii) any goodwill attached to the demised premises by reason of the carrying on thereof of the business of the tenant its sub-tenants or their predecessors in title in their respective businesses and

(iii) any increase in rental value of the demised premises attributable to the existence at the relevant review date of any improvement to the demised premises or any part thereof carried out with consent where required other-wise than in pursuance of an obligation to the landlord or its predecessors in title

either (a) by the tenant its sub tenants or their respective predecessors in title during the said term or during any period of occupation prior thereto arising out of an agreement to grant such term

or (b) by any tenant or sub-tenant of the demised premises before the commencement of the term hereby granted so long as the landlord or its predecessors in title have not since the improvement was carried out had vacant possession of the relevant part of the demised premises

[AND the improvement was completed not more than twenty-one years before the relevant review date]

NOTE 3.
Paragraph (B) (iii) (b) may be applicable only on a renewal. Additionally the words in square brackets may be omitted or amended if the twenty-one year period is not appropriate.

107

CLAUSE 4.

Further provisions as to arbitration *(see Note 4)*

IT IS HEREBY FURTHER PROVIDED in relation to said revised rent as follows:

(A) *(in the case of arbitration)* the arbitration shall be conducted in accordance with the Arbitration Act 1950 or any statutory modification or re-enactment thereof for the time being in force

As to independent valuation *(see Note 4)*

(B) *(in the case of determination by a valuer)*

(i) the fees and expenses of the valuer including the cost of his appointment shall be borne equally by the landlord and the tenant who shall otherwise each bear their own costs and

(ii) *the valuer shall afford to each of the parties hereto an opportunity to make representations to him and*

(iii) if the valuer shall die, delay or become unwilling or incapable of acting or if for any other reason the president for the time being of the Royal Institution of Chartered Surveyors or the person acting on his behalf shall in his absolute discretion think fit he may be writing discharge the valuer and appoint another in his place

As to the memoranda of ascertainment

(C) When the amount of any rent to be ascertained as hereinbefore provided shall have been so ascertained memoranda thereof shall thereupon be signed by or on behalf of the landlord and the tenant and annexed to this lease and counterpart thereof and the parties shall bear their own costs in respect thereof

NOTE 4.

If the first version of Clause 3 is used (arbitrator or independent valuer) both (A) and (B) apply. If the second version (arbitrator) is used (B) should be omitted and if the third version (independent valuer) is used (A) should be omitted. (B) (ii) is optional as regards an independent valuer.

NOTE 5.

The words in italics should be omitted if the reviews are "upwards only".

NOTE 6.

The words in italics should be included if the reviews are "upward only".

As to interim payment and final adjustments (see Note 5)

As to notice by the tenant where appointment of arbitrator or independnet valuer is at the landlord's option (see Note 6)

(D) (i) if the revised rent payable on and from any review date has not been agreed by that review date rent shall continue to be payable at the rate previously payable and forthwith upon the revised rent being ascertained the tenant shall pay to the landlord any shortfall between the rent and the revised rent *or as the case may be the landlord shall pay to the tenant any excess of the rent paid over the revised rent* payable up to and on the preceding quarter day

(ii) for the purposes of this proviso the revised rent shall be deemed to have been ascertained on the date when the same has been agreed between the parties or as the case may be the date of the award of the arbitrator or of the determination by the valuer

(E) Whenever a revised rent in respect of any review period has not been agreed between the landlord and the tenant before the relevant review date and the landlord has not made any application to the president for the time being of the Royal Institution of Chartered Surveyors as hereinbefore provided the tenant may serve on the landlord notice in writing containing a proposal as to the amount of such revised rent *not being less than the rent payable immediately before the commencement of the relevant review period* and the amount so proposed shall be deemed to have been agreed by the parties as the revised rent for the relevant review period and sub-clause

(D) (i) hereof shall apply accordingly unless the landlord shall make such application as aforesaid within three months after service of such notice by the tenant

109

7.3 TERMS AND ASSUMPTIONS

The basis for operating a rent review is provided by the terms of the lease. Some contain provisions that are simple, even naïve, whilst others are of frightening complexity. The outcome has been a sustained bout of litigation resulting in a considerable body of advice, much of which is of real assistance to those concerned in managing the landlord and tenant relationship.

The following notes report the main areas of difficulty and the manner of their resolution: though the decided cases provide a useful route it should not be supposed that all problems have been overcome.

7.3.1 Basis of rent to be assessed

The rent is variously described as being 'open market rental value', 'rack rental value', 'full market rent', 'reasonable market rent' and others.

It is doubtful whether there is a significant difference in these terms or that different values could be ascribed to them although in Cuff *v*. J. & F. Stone Ltd, Megarry J. suggested a difference between 'reasonable rent' and 'open market rent' with these words:

'The word 'reasonable' no doubt requires the surveyor to reject a rent which though obtainable in the open market by reason of special circumstances, appears to him to exceed the rent for the premises which is right and fair: but I do not think it does more than that.'

Other stipulated matters such as length of lease remaining unexpired and user will tend to affect the rental value.

Where a lease provided for a revision of the rent after five years but no formula or machinery was included in the lease for determining the rent in default of agreement, the court held that, as it would be unfair for the parties to receive no rent after the first period there would be implied a term that in default of agreement an arbitrator should be appointed to fix the rent on the basis of a market rent (Thomas Bates & Son Ltd *v*. Wyndham's (Lingerie) Ltd).

7.3.2 Time limits

It was once thought that unless time limits contained in clauses relating to the procedure for initiating rent reviews were observed strictly, the opportunity of obtaining a higher rent would be lost.

The rapid increase in rental values served only to make the landlords more anxious to receive their share. Lord Salmon understood the problem and expressed it in these terms

> 'In a period of acute inflation, such as has been experienced for the last 20 years or so, and might well be experienced for many years to come, what was a fair market rent at the date when a lease was granted would probably become wholly uneconomic within a few years. Tenants who were anxious for security of tenure required a term of reasonable duration, often 21 years or more. Landlords, on the other hand, were unwilling to grant such leases unless they contained rent revision clauses which would enable the rent to be raised at regular intervals to what was then the fair market rent of the property demised. Accordingly, it has become the practice for all long leases to contain a rent revision clause providing for a revision of the rent every so many years. Leases used to provide for such revision to be made every 10 years. Now [1977] the period is normally every seven and not infrequently every five years. It is totally unrealistic to regard such clauses as conferring a privilege upon the landlord or as imposing a burden upon the tenant.'

The time limits concern the notice which has to be given by the parties to 'trigger' the review procedure, to reply to proposals made under it or to take steps to have the new amount determined where the parties are unable to agree. There are no statutory provisions relating to the content of rent review clauses and the courts are not concerned in their determination. In the event of a disagreement between the parties as to the legal interpretation of a rent review clause, the courts have a part to play: provision for reference to a third party is usually provided where the only question is one of value as is more usually the case.

(a) *Where time is not 'of the essence'*

Fraser L. J. examined the need to adhere to time limits laid down in the lease in Samuel Properties (Developments) Ltd *v.* Hayek and expressed his opinion

'... that the equitable rule against treating time as the essence of a contract is applicable to rent review clauses unless there is some special reason for excluding its application to a particular clause.'

The case of C. H. Bailey Ltd *v.* Memorial Enterprises Ltd concerned the construction of a rent review clause where it was provided that the market rental value was to be found *on* a certain date. The tenant contended that as it was not determined on that date (indeed it was not ascertained until some 3½ years later) it was not payable. The court held that the provision did not prevent the rent being ascertained at some later date and that the new rent was payable from the date of the rent review.

The cases of United Scientific Holdings Ltd *v.* Burnley Borough Council, and Cheapside Land Development Co. Ltd and others *v.* Messels Service Co. (taken together by the House of Lords) proved to be the watershed of 'time of the essence' cases and provided Diplock L. J. with the opportunity to review the more important of the earlier relevant decisions and to express the hope that it would reduce the number of occasions on which it would be necessary to have recourse to the courts in order to ascertain whether delay had deprived the landlord of his right.

In the United Scientific Holdings case, it was held that unless the lease contained any contrary indications there was a presumption that the time-table laid down in a rent review clause was *not* of the essence of the contract and that the review rent could therefore be determined outside the dates laid down by the lease. Salmon L. J. said

'These [rent review] provisions as to time are not in my opinion mandatory or inflexible: they are only directory ... A mandatory provision is one which must be fulfilled in all its strictness and failure to perform it means that the whole thing fails, whereas a directory provision does not require that degree of strictness: even though it is not complied with, the whole does not fail. It could still be regarded as valid and effective.'

The Cheapside case contained 'an elaborate time-table' as to what was to be done in various eventualities including provisions in respect of persons over whom neither had any control whilst at some stages progress of the procedure was within the exclusive control of the landlord. The court held that the provisions for review were not of the essence and that, once fixed, the rent for the period from the review date could be recovered by the landlord.

Where a clause in a lease provided the timetable for service on the tenant of a notice to agree the rent and went on

'... provided always that any failure to give or receive such notice shall not render void the right of the landlord hereunder to require the agreement or determination as aforesaid of a new rent'

Megan L. J. was in no doubt that a notice served after the last date provided in the clause did not prevent the landlord from validly demanding agreement or arbitration of a new rent (Kenilworth Industrial Sites Ltd *v.* E. C. Little & Co. Ltd). One of the judges in a later case thought that the Kenilworth case was probably the origin of the unfortunate dichotomy between review clauses which conferred an option and those which merely provided machinery. In Accuba Ltd *v.* Allied Shoe Repairs Ltd a similar decision was given, the stipulations as to time being classified as 'mere machinery'.

In Vince and Another *v.* Alps Hotel Ltd and Another the terms of the lease for the agreement of a new rent for the second seven year period of the lease were not complied with within the times specified. Nearly two years after the review date, the landlord's attention was drawn to the United Scientific Holdings Ltd decision as a result of which they claimed a declaration that the review provisions could be operated retrospectively. The defendants asserted that time was of the essence and that the plaintiffs' conduct in allowing them to incur substantial expenditure in the belief that the rent would not be increased estopped them from asserting that time was not of the essence. It was held that the plaintiffs could not pursue their rights until they knew of the decision (which was a change in the law as then understood) and that there was no evidence that the defendants relied on the plaintiffs' silence. The plaintiffs obtained the declaration sought.

The plaintiffs in Dean and Chapter of Chichester *v*. Lennards Ltd served a notice in accordance with the terms of the rent review clause except that it did not meet the requirement that any such notice should state 'the suggested new rent reserved.' Denning L. J. remarked that the clause should not fail and be held invalid 'simply because of the omission of one bit of machinery'.

(b) *Where time is 'of the essence'*

One of the most helpful observations was made by Fraser L. J. when he said

> 'The rule [that time not ordinarily being of the essence] would of course be excluded if the review clause expressly stated that time was to be of the essence. It would also be excluded if the context clearly indicated that that was the intention of the parties, as for instance where the tenant had a right to break the lease by notice given by a specified date which was later than the last date for serving the landlord's trigger notice. The tenant's notice to determine the contract would be one where the time limit was mandatory and the necessary implication is that the time limit for giving the landlord's notice of review must also be mandatory.'

In spite of the hope expressed by Lord Diplock in the United Scientific Holdings case, activity continues on the question of the status of the time requirements of the review process.

In Drebbond Ltd *v*. Horsham District Council the rent review clause provided for the rent to be adjusted and if agreement was not reached a reference to a sole arbitrator

> ' . . . by notice in writing given to the tenant within three months thereafter but not otherwise'.

The 'trigger notice', setting off the procedure, was given in accordance with the timetable but the 'arbitration notice' was not. It was held that the way in which the requirement was expressed showed the time limit to be obligatory and not merely indicative and to operate so as to make time of the essence.

A lease made lengthy and detailed provisions for rent review ending with paragraph (5)

'All stipulations as to time in the foregoing subclause . . . shall be of the essence of the contract and shall not be capable of enlargement save as agreed in writing by the parties.'

The landlord wrote in accordance with the provisions of the lease proposing a rent from the review date of £5250 per annum to which the tenant replied:

'We formally acknowledge receipt of your notice of rent review for the above property and we would hardly need to add that we do not accept your revised figure.'

No further steps were taken by the tenant until after the time limit set for agreement or service of a counternotice had expired. It was held that the tenant's letter contained nothing sufficiently specific to constitute a counternotice and judgment was given in favour of the landlord (Bellinger *v*. South London Stationers Ltd).

A similar case was Oldschool and Another *v*. Johns where the lease provided that in the absence of agreement, a counternotice was to be served by a certain date requiring determination of value by an independent surveyor (time to be of the essence thereof). A letter from the tenant's solicitors disputing the rental value and asking for evidence in support of the landlord's proposed rent was held to be at the best ambiguous and in any event not an effective counternotice. It was further held that certain actions of the landlord did not constitute waiver or estoppel.

In Amalgamated Estates Ltd *v*. Joystretch Manufacturing Ltd it was held that a landlord's notice specifying a new rent need not be a bona fide and genuine pre-estimate of the rent and that a tenant's reply to the notice in which he disagreed with the proposed increase and made a request for an explanation of the basis of the landlord's proposal was not a counternotice. All the stipulations were subject to time being of the essence.

It was pointed out that in such cases it is possible for the tenant to apply to the High Court for an extension of time for the commencement of arbitration proceedings which may be granted where the court is of opinion that undue hardship would otherwise be caused.

Another case where time was stated to be of the essence was Weller *v.* Akehurst where it was held that when the provisions for ascertaining open market value were defined with precision and were required to be effected in a particular way, the provision as to time being of the essence defeated the landlord. Having failed to observe the timetable, he was unable to obtain a review to the open market value. In these circumstances it was held that the original rent should continue. But in Thomas Bates & Son Ltd *v.* Wyndhams (Lingerie) Ltd where the lease provided no machinery for fixing the rent on review it was said that there was no difficulty in implying a term that a market rent should be fixed.

Four further cases of interest have been reported recently. In C. Bradley & Sons Ltd *v.* Telefusion Ltd the lease provided that time was of the essence but it was uncertain as to whether it applied to the whole of the clause or only to parts of it. It was held that it was intended that time should be of the essence for the arbitrator to make his determination and, as he did not do so, the landlord was out of time.

In Edlingham Ltd *v.* MFI Furniture Centres Ltd time was again stated to be of the essence in a rent review clause. In reply to the landlord's notice specifying a new rent in accordance with the clause the defendant company's company secretary acknowledged receipt of the notice, stated that the suggested rent was considered excessive and requested the comparables on which it was based. It was held that the letter was not effective as a counternotice and therefore that the new rent was properly due (and see 'Oldschool' above). Again, there was some discussion of the possibility of the tenant applying under section 27 of the *Arbitration Act 1950* for leave to proceed despite the lapse of time: however, the aggrieved party is required to persuade the court that in the circumstances of the case undue hardship would be caused if leave was withheld.

A further question of construction was raised in Al Saloom *v* Shirley James Travel Service Ltd. The case was concerned with whether the landlord had served notice in accordance

with the requirements of the clause in the lease which contained provisions about break and review procedures. It was
held that as the two provisions were closely allied to one
another, the same interpretation must apply to each. Diplock
L. J. was quoted as saying there was a practical business
reason for treating time as of the essence of a break clause.
It was held that the phrase must mean the same in relation
to each clause and therefore that time must also be treated
as of the essence of the review clause.

In Rahman and others *v.* Kenshire the rent review clause
and a break clause were interrelated: there was no question
but that time was of the essence in the break clause and
again it was held that it must also be of the essence in the
review clause. The intention of the document appeared to
be to give the tenant an opportunity to determine the tenancy
after the review rent was known: the intention would not be
achieved unless both clauses were treated in the same way.

There is some evidence that the elaborate clauses designed
to avoid the various pitfalls of the rent review arena have not
been entirely successful.

7.3.3 Restrictions as to user

Where the lease limits the user in some way, the rent must
be assessed with regard to that restriction which will often
(but not always) produce a lower rent for the landlord.

In one case there was a restriction on use to offices in
connection with the lessee's business of Consulting Engineers.
The arbitrator was urged to take into account a possible
relaxation of the terms of the user clause. He stated a case
for the court which held that he must make an award on the
basis of the user clause and not any variation which either
party might be prepared to agree to (Plinth Property Investments *v.* Mott, Hay and Anderson where the rent was found
to be £130355 per annum without the user restriction and
£89200 per annum with the restriction).

In the course of his judgment Brandon L. J. said in relation
to the contention that the landlord would be prepared to
relax the restrictions:

'What the arbitrator has to consider is what those rights
and obligations are on either side and assess the rent in

the light of them. He is not to say to himself "Those who have rights may not enforce them and those who have obligations may not be required to enforce them". He is to assume that the rights will be enforced and the obligations will be performed. He is to look at the legal position of the parties and nothing else'.

The Court of Appeal had no hesitation in ruling that a possible future use in breach of planning control was not a matter to be taken into account when assessing the review rent.

But where the review rent was to be assessed on the basis of the open market rental ignoring any statutory restrictions it was held that the flats included in the lease were to be valued disregarding the possibility of the rents being subject to a ceiling fixed by the Rent Officer (Langham House Developments Ltd *v*. Brompton Securities Ltd).

An unusual lease provision was considered in Trust House Forte Albany Hotels Ltd *v*. Daejan Investments Ltd where it was provided that parts of the demised premises used as a hotel were to be valued as if they were let for retail purposes. The landlords contended that the clause required the further assumption that the premises were in a state suitable for such use but this contention was not upheld.

7.3.4   Provisions as to unexpired term

In an endeavour to avoid the possibility of lower rental values being fixed as a result of the limited term available, some leases seek to overcome the problem by providing for specific assumptions.

In Pivot Properties Ltd *v*. Secretary of State for the Environment the lease provided for the 'rack rental market value' to be fixed on review, being 'the best rent at which the demised premises might reasonably be expected to let in the open market for a term not exceeding 5½ years'.

The arbitrator made alternative awards: if any extension available under the *Landlord and Tenant Act 1954* was to be reflected, the rental value was £2 925 000, otherwise it was £2 100 000. The Court held that the possibility of extension was to be taken into account.

It is common to provide that vacant possession is to be assumed when assessing rental value on review.

In the recent case of Avon County Council *v.* Alliance Property Company Ltd the Court looked at the background to the original lease (even though both parties had been superseded) and concluded that the rent was related to land and buildings and not to the leasehold interests and that it was possible to imply a vacant possession basis even though such a stipulation was not contained in the head lease and the property was subject to a number of sub-leases and licences.

7.3.5   Treatment of tenants' improvements

The status of tenant's improvements on renewals is made clear by the 1954 Act: subject to certain qualifications such improvements are ignored by the court in fixing the rent under the new lease. On review, however, the intention of the parties will suggest the basis and that intention will be found primarily in the lease. Two interesting cases on this point are Cuff *v.* J. and F. Stone Lighting Ltd 1978 and Ponsford *v.* HMS Aerosols Ltd.

In Cuff the tenants carried out some alterations to increase the floor area during the currency of their 21 year lease. The tenants obtained a statutory renewal at the end of that lease for the maximum term of 14 years and a rent review was incorporated to operate at the end of the seventh year. The rent under the new lease ignored the rental value of the tenant's improvements but when the rent fell to be reviewed the landlord claimed an amount to include the value of the improvements. He was held to be entitled to a rent on that basis as the review clause referred to 'a reasonable rent for the demised premises' the point being that the improvements carried out by the tenants had become part of those premises and were therefore, in the absence of a specific provision in the lease, to be included in the assessment of a reasonable rent.

In the Ponsford case, a serious fire occurred a year after a 21 year lease had been granted to the tenant. The premises were rebuilt and the landlord agreed to substantial improvements being incorporated by the tenant at his expense — the not inconsiderable sum of £31 780. Within five years of rebuilding a review took place and the landlord claimed a rent to include the rental value of the improvements. The court upheld the landlord's claim and drew attention to Cuff (previously unreported). It is clear that the statutory disregard in section 34 cannot be imported into a review clause, the presumption being that the parties strike the bargain they intend. The case was decided by a 3—2 majority in the House of Lords. While it is difficult to see how any other decision could have been reached on the facts, it is doubtful whether such a situation was intended by the legislators. It is ironic to reflect that when the lease ends in 1989, the tenant will be in a position to claim a new lease at a rent which disregards the effect of his improvements.

A difficult case of tenant's improvements was considered in GREA Real Property Investment Ltd *v.* Williams 1979. The tenant took a bare shell being the third floor of an office block and proceeded to carry out all the remaining building works including partitions, lavatories, cloakrooms and so on. The first six months of the lease was at a peppercorn. The review clause provided for the disregard of any effect on the rental value of any improvement carried out by the tenants, their works of fitting out and finishing being referred to specifically in this exclusion. On review, the landlord's valuer estimated the rental value of the completed suite and deducted a percentage for the tenant's improvements while the tenant's valuer deducted the annual equivalent of the updated cost of the improvements from the rental value. As a result of a consultative case from the arbitrator, the judge advised him — among other things — that the intention of the parties had been to credit the tenant with the rental equivalent of the updated cost but with nothing else. In the course of his consideration he made some helpful general points of interest to valuers, including a reference to the difference between cost and value though he refrained from expressing a view as to the valuation method to be used in arriving at the rental value.

The same judge had this to say in a later case.

'Now this court is not a valuer. All I can do is to say whether there is an error on the face of the award and there will be such an error if a method of valuation is adopted which clearly does not follow the intention of the parties. I can say, therefore, whether a method of valuation is wrong, but not necessarily what method of valuation is right' (Forbes J. Estates Projects Ltd *v.* Greenwich London Borough Council 1979).

7.3.6 Restrictions on assignment

Leases often contain an absolute or conditional prohibition of assignment of the unexpired term of the lease. The precise effect of the restriction on rental value needs to be considered in the light of the practical effect on the marketability of the lease.

A clause requiring the tenant to offer to surrender the lease to his landlord before proceeding with any assignment to a third party was held to be contrary to section 38 of the *Landlord and Tenant Act 1954*. This was so, even though there were provisions for the landlord to match the payment offered by the prospective assignee (Allnatt (London) Properties Ltd *v.* Newton).

7.3.7 Profitability of tenant's business

The tenant cannot be required to produce his books of account under normal circumstances, a proposisition recently confirmed by W. J. Barton Ltd *v.* Long Acre Securities Ltd. However, it was held in Harewood Hotels Ltd *v.* Harris that evidence of accounts was admissible in showing the reasonable open market rent likely to be achieved whilst in St. Martin's Theatre, in *re*: Bright Enterprises Ltd *v.* Lord Willoughby de Broke, it was held that the tenant could be required to produce his accounts.

7.4 THIRD PARTY PROCEEDINGS

Any provision for the review of rent during the course of a lease must anticipate that there will be times when the parties cannot reach agreement on the new rent. There is a need for the lease to contain machinery to enable the dispute to be resolved and it is normal to provide for the appointment of a third party, usually a surveyor, to act as arbitrator or expert (or independent valuer as he is referred to in the RICS Guidance Notes on this topic).

Where an arbitrator is appointed he will conduct the proceedings in a formal manner much in line with court procedures. Where a point of law is at issue he may, with the agreement of the parties, sit with a legal assessor or seek legal advice.

He may take evidence orally or in writing: evidence is likely to include valuation calculations and analyses of comparables. The evidence may be tested by cross-examination and re-examination and it is usual for the arbitrator to inspect the subject property and the comparables as far as is possible.

Where required by the parties or by the instrument appointing him, his award must be reasoned. He may find it appropriate to make alternative awards where the result turns on a point of law.

Unless excluded by agreement the parties have a right of appeal to the High Court subject to obtaining leave of the court.

Fees may be fixed by agreement with the arbitrator when he is first appointed or may be based on the amount of his award. They may fall equally on the parties, follow the award (so that the unsuccessful party is responsible for payment) or be shared in the discretion of the arbitrator. Either party may apply to have the arbitrator's fees taxed by the court.

In recent times there has been a tendency for the expert to replace the arbitrator.

The expert is much more reliant on his own judgment and is not even bound to hear the parties unless they reserve the right to appear.

The advantages claimed for the appointment of an expert are that the procedure is quicker and less cumbersome and therefore cheaper: that it is preferable, where the parties' representatives have been unable to resolve the issues, to have a completely fresh approach and that the expert is liable to the parties in negligence.

It is too early to gauge whether such advantages outweigh the opportunity for ordered presentation of evidence and cross examination of witnesses. One important consideration is that the precise nature of the dispute is usually unknown when the procedures for resolving differences are laid down by the lease.

7.5 IMPLEMENTATION

More often than not the property manager serves the appropriate notices to commence the review procedure and then proceeds to negotiate the rent payable on review. Although there has been a flood of litigation on this subject the vast majority of reviews has been concluded, if not amicably, at least without recourse to the courts or to third party proceedings.

When agreement has been reached on the review rent it has the effect of introducing a new term into the existing lease and the parties' solicitors should take the necessary action: as there is no intention to create a new tenancy the terms of the agreement may be endorsed on the existing lease. A new lease is unnecessary. The point is important: an endorsement noting an agreed variation in the terms of an existing lease is not a lease for stamp duty purposes but a bond or covenant subject to section 64(i)(a) of the *Finance Act 1971*. The *ad valorem* scale of duty is appreciably lower than the stamp duty on leases: both may be found in Table 11.5.

FURTHER READING

Baum, A. (1983) *Statutory Valuations*, Routledge and Kegan Paul, London.
Bernstein, R. (1981) *Handbook of Rent Review*, Butterworths, London.

CHAPTER 8

Residential tenancies

8.1 INTRODUCTION

Amendments to rent control in 1980 came three years after
the most recent consolidating Act and 65 years after the
initial steps were taken to control rents and provide security
of tenure at the beginning of the First World War. The legislation has been prolific, complicated, often partisan and largely
unsuccessful.

The purpose of the Rent Acts has been well described by
Scarman L. J. in Horford Investments Ltd *v*. Lambert 1973
where he said

> 'The policy of the Rent Acts was and is to protect the
> tenant in his home, whether the threat be to extort a
> premium for the grant or renewal of his tenancy, to increase
> his rent or to evict him. It is not a policy for the protection
> of an entrepreneur such as the defendant whose interest
> is exclusively commercial, that is to say, to obtain from
> his tenants a greater rental income than the rent which
> he has contracted to pay his landlord. The Rent Acts have
> throughout their history constituted an interference with
> contract and property rights for a specific purpose —
> the redress of the balance of advantage enjoyed in a world
> of housing shortage by the landlord over those who have
> to rent their homes.'

Today, few would argue that the less privileged in the community should live in substandard accommodation, be in
fear of eviction or be expected to house themselves to a
satisfactory standard without some assistance. But the

spectacle of the consistent failure of successive governments to achieve even modest success in the housing field suggests that control and restriction of the private sector is not the solution. There is reason to believe that, given the assurance of a stable market and economic rents, the private sector would respond to the demand. The residential housing market is the only investment area where the investor has been forced through restrictive legislation to accept an uncertain and inadequate return on capital coupled with, for the most part, enforced contracts.

It is arguable that a government subsidy of the difference between the market rent and the rent which the tenant could afford in his circumstances, would be no more expensive to the Exchequer and achieve better results than have resulted from the direct involvement of the public sector in the provision of subsidized accommodation.

Most residential tenancies are subject to some form of direction, the principal relevant legislation being the *Rent Act* and the *Protection from Eviction Act*, both passed in 1977 and the *Housing Act 1980*.

It is intended to describe the scope of the protection available; to set out, briefly, the circumstances under which some tenancies may be outside the provisions of the Acts and then to discuss the types of tenancy, the limitation of rents, security of tenure and the procedure for registration and phasing of rents. New forms of tenancy, responsibility for repairs, the assessment of service charges and provisions for subletting, premiums and notices will follow and the chapter will end with short notes on improvement grants and licences.

8.2 THE TENANCIES AFFECTED

The legislation has set up an elaborate system of protection: the different forms it may take will be considered but first the type of occupation affected will be considered briefly. Section 1 of Part I of the 1977 Act provides that

'subject to this part of the Act, a tenancy under which a dwelling house (which may be a house or part of a house) is let as a separate dwelling is a protected tenancy for the purposes of this Act' while section 152(1) provides that a tenancy includes a sub-tenancy.

The section refers to tenancies and the protection available to a licensee is different and more limited. The distinction between a tenancy and a licence has been discussed in Chapter 5 but further consideration to licences in the context of rent control legislation is given later in this chapter.

There is no definition of 'dwelling-house' beyond the explanatory note in parentheses in the section. It may be that the practical difficulties of providing a satisfactory definition encouraged the draughtsman to leave the problem for resolution by the courts in the circumstances of the particular case. 'It must be a question of fact whether premises are a house or not': as Bankes L. J. said in *Epsom Grand Stand Association Ltd v. Clarke*, 1919

> 'if the agreement is to let a barn, the tenant even though he lives there cannot be heard to say it is let as a dwelling-house'

8.2.1 Protected tenancies

The distinguishing feature of a protected tenancy is that it springs from and follows a contractual tenancy. Certain types of tenancy are excepted from the provisions relating to protected tenancies and are set out in sections 4 to 16.

The general proposition is that a letting of a dwelling-house as a separate dwelling is a protected tenancy. The exceptions are given below.

(a) *Dwelling-houses above certain rateable values (section 4)*

The rateable value at a certain date exceeds a certain figure: different ceilings apply according as to what is the 'appropriate day' and as to whether the dwelling is in Greater London or elsewhere.

There are rules for determining the appropriate day: for most purposes it is to be 23 March 1965 but where the dwelling was not in the valuation list at that date the earliest appearance in the list is the date to be adopted. Should the list be altered so as to affect the rateable value on the appropriate day, the amendment prevails.

Table 8.1 sets out the rateable value limits and other

information and the opportunity is taken to include information required for section 5 (tenancies at low rents) and section 19 (restricted contracts).

(b) *Tenancies at low rents (section 5)*

No rent is payable or the rent payable is less than two-thirds of the rateable value on the appropriate day. (The provisions as to date and area are included in Table 8.1) 'Rent' will be the total amount payable including any payment in respect of rates: if the rent is reduced to reflect services performed by the tenant, the reduced amount is the figure which will be used to determine whether the tenancy is a protected one. Where the tenancy is for a term certain exceeding 21 years (a 'long tenancy') the rent shall be determined after the deduction of any amount expressed to be payable in respect of rates, services, repairs, maintenance or insurance.

(c) *Dwelling-houses let with other land (section 6)*

This exception as set out by section 6 and interpreted in the courts provides that any land or premises let together with a dwelling-house shall be treated as part of the dwelling-house where that use is the dominant purpose of the letting or where it consists of agricultural land exceeding two acres in extent.

(d) *Payments for board or attendance (section 7)*

The exception does not operate unless the amount of rent which is fairly attributable to attendance, having regard to the value of the attendance to the tenant, forms a substantial part of the whole rent. There is no such requirement in respect of board. But the tenancy may be protected as a restricted contract.

(e) *Lettings to students (section 8)*

The student must be pursuing, or intending to pursue, a course of study provided by a specified educational institution and having a tenancy granted by that institution or another specified institution or body of persons. *The Protected Tenancies (Exceptions) Regulations 1974* (SI No. 1366) lists the types of institution and the *Restricted Tenan-*

cies (Further Exceptions) Regulations 1976 (SI No. 905) lists
the specific institutions within the scope of this exception.

(f) *Holiday lettings (section 9)*

It should be noted that this section relates to a tenancy
where the purpose is to confer on the tenant the right to
occupy the dwelling-house for a holiday without the landlord being in danger of creating a protected tenancy. No
definition of 'holiday' is provided.

(g) *Agricultural holdings (section 10)*

The exception refers to a tenancy of an agricultural holding
within the meaning of the *Agricultural Holdings Act 1948*
where the holding is occupied by the person responsible for
the control of the farming (tenant or as servant or agent for
tenant).

(h) *Licensed premises (section 11)*

The exception applies to on-licences, which also escape the
provisions of Part II of the *Landlord and Tenant Act 1954*.
The exception does not apply to off-licences in cases where
there is some living accommodation within the definition
of 'dwelling-house'.

(i) *Resident landlords (section 12, amended)*

A tenancy of a dwelling-house granted after 28 November
1980 is excepted if

'(a) the dwelling-house forms part only of a building
      including part only of a flat in a purpose-built block
      of flats ('flat' is defined as a dwelling-house which
      forms part only of a building and is separated hori-
      zontally from another dwelling-house which forms
      part of the same building) and
 (b) the tenancy was granted by a person who, at the time
      that he granted it, occupied as his residence another
      dwelling-house which also forms part of the building
      and
 (c) at all times since the tenancy was granted the interest
      of the landlord under the tenancy has belonged to

a person who, at the time he owned that interest, occupied as his residence another dwelling-house which also formed part of that building'.

(Breaks of occupation of up to one year are permitted depending on the circumstances: the most important event is, perhaps, a sale by the landlord in which case a break of more than twenty-eight days will be fatal to continuation of the exception, unless the purchaser notifies the tenant in writing of his intention to occupy as a residence in which case his rights will be preserved for up to six months). The exception does not affect the rights of a tenant previously occupying as a protected or statutory tenant or where a term of years certain is granted to a tenant who occupied earlier but not as a protected tenant. The latter provision defeats the landlord in any attempt to avoid the jurisdiction of the Rent Assessment Committee.

Where the landlord is no longer resident and is not within the provisions of (a) above, the tenancy becomes a protected tenancy: if the tenant is under notice to quit which had been served and extended because of a reference to the Rent Assessment Committee but had not expired before the date on which the tenancy became a protected tenancy then the notice is to expire on the following day when the tenancy will become a statutory tenancy.

(j) *Landlord's interest belonging to the Crown (section 73)*

Certain types of Crown tenant may become regulated tenants. They are tenants of the Duchies of Lancaster and Cornwall and tenants of the Crown Estate Commissioners. There are consequential provisions relating to the grounds for possession and to lawful premiums.

Similar provisions are made for occupiers of agricultural tied accommodation who may now become statutory tenants. Tenants of the Sovereign's private estates or of a government department are not included in these provisions.

(k) *Other exceptions*

Other exceptions refer to dwelling-houses where the landlord's interest belongs to a local authority, housing association or housing co-operative and are therefore beyond the scope of this work.

(l) *General philosophy*

The general philosophy of the legislation is to provide security of tenure and limited rent levels for the tenant: many of the exceptions outlined above are intended to give relief to the landlord in certain limited directions while at the same time avoiding the creation of loopholes by which the legislation is made less effective. It is not surprising, therefore, that the exceptions are detailed and laborious: any particular case should be considered by reference to the wording of the Act (sections 4 to 16 and Schedule 12, the latter as amended by the *Housing Act 1980*)

8.2.2 Security of tenure

A central feature of the legislation is that there is security of tenure whether the tenancy is protected or statutory. A notice to quit is of no effect unless the landlord has obtained an order of court: the court shall not make an order for possession unless it considers it reasonable to do so and that either

(a) The court is satisfied that suitable alternative accommodation is available for the tenant or will be available for him when the order takes effect or
(b) The circumstances are as specified in any of the Cases in Part I of Schedule 15 of the 1977 Act (with later additions and one repeal there is now a total of nineteen cases)

Where the tenancy has a contractual base, the landlord must first serve a valid notice to quit (valid, that is, in relation between the parties) and which must in any event be in writing, give certain prescribed information and give not less than four weeks' notice.

Where the landlord has a right of re-entry or forfeiture under a lease he can exercise it only by proceedings in court while any person is lawfully residing in the premises or part of the premises. The courts have very wide discretion in deciding what is reasonable. In deciding whether alternative accommodation is suitable the courts have on numerous occasions considered the requirements of the particular rather than the hypothetical tenant. The landlord may offer the tenant as alternative accommodation *part* of the existing demised premises (e.g. the dwelling-house and part only of the garden or part of the living accommodation presently occupied by him).

Guidance is given in Part IV of Schedule 15 where it is provided that the accommodation shall be deemed to be suitable if it consists of either

(a) Premises which are to be let as a separate dwelling such that they will then be let on a protected tenancy or
(b) Premises to be let as a separate dwelling on terms which will, in the opinion of the courts, afford to the tenant security of tenure reasonably equivalent to that offered in the case of a protected tenancy —

where the accommodation is reasonably suitable to the needs of the tenant and his family as regards proximity to place of work and either suitable to the means and needs of the tenant and his family as regards extent and character or similar as regards rental and extent to any dwelling-houses provided in the neighbourhood by any housing authority for persons with similar needs. Where housing is to be provided by the housing authority for the district a certificate of that authority to the effect that suitable alternative accommodation will be provided by a date specified is to be regarded as conclusive evidence.

8.2.3 Statutory tenancies

The terms, conditions and rules of succession of the statutory tenancy are laid down by sections 2 and 3 and Schedule I of the 1977 Act.

Section 2 provides in part that

'(a) after the termination of a protected tenancy of a dwelling-house the person who, immediately before that termination, was the protected tenant of the dwelling-house shall, if and so long as he occupies the dwelling-house as his residence, be the statutory tenant of it; and

(b)   Part I of Schedule I to this Act shall have effect for
      determining what person (if any) is the statutory
      tenant of a dwelling-house at any time after the death
      of a person who, immediately before his death, was
      either a protected tenant of the dwelling-house or the
      statutory tenant of it by virtue of paragraph (a) above.'

The status of statutory tenant is accorded to former protected tenants and to any person who qualifies as a successor
on death of the tenant. The statutory tenant enjoys this
personal right only so long as he remains in occupation
(though the courts have given a broad interpretation to temporary absence and distinguished that from non-occupation).
He has no right to assign or sub-let the whole, whatever the
original agreement may have provided though he may sub-
let part and still retain protection under the Act but perhaps
not in respect of the part sub-let: in such circumstances,
however, the sub-tenant will usually gain protection under
the Act.

Section 3 provides in part

'(1) So long as he retains possession, a statutory tenant
      shall observe and be entitled to the benefit of all the
      terms and conditions of the original contract of
      tenancy, so far as they are consistent with the pro-
      visions of this Act.'

It has been held that an option to purchase the reversion
'at any time' contained in a lease expires when the original
tenancy ceases to exist: i.e. it is not carried over to the statutory tenancy.

A statutory tenant is required by section 5 of the *Protection from Eviction Act 1977* to give not less than four weeks'
notice to quit and longer where so required by the original
contract of tenancy. Where no notice was required under that
contract, the tenant must give not less than three months'
notice. In either case, the notice must be served so as to expire at the end of a rental period. It is provided also that the
landlord shall be entitled to access for inspection and to
reasonable facilities for executing any repairs. Part II of
Schedule I refers to relinquishing tenancies and changing
tenants.

A statutory tenant is entitled to receive payment from his landlord as a condition of giving up possession but it is an offence to ask for or receive any payment from any one other than the landlord. Similarly, the purchase of any furniture as a condition of giving up possession is to be at a reasonable price, any excess to be treated as a payment asked for as a condition of giving up possession.

There is provision for a statutory tenant to be replaced by an incoming tenant who is to be deemed the statutory tenant from the transfer date. In order to be effective the landlord must be a party to the agreement which must be in writing. The rights of succession are limited. It is an offence to require a payment for entering into such an agreement, except that the outgoing tenant can ask for payment of outgoings referable to any period after the transfer date, his reasonable expenditure on structural alterations or fixtures which he is not entitled to remove, any sum paid by him to his predecessor and, where part of the dwelling is used for business, trade or professional purposes, a reasonable amount in respect of goodwill.

A statutory tenancy may also arise from succession. The spouse of the original statutory tenant becomes the statutory tenant provided that he or she was residing with the tenant immediately before his or her death. Where there is no qualifying spouse, a member of the tenant's family who was residing with him at the time and for a period of six months immediately before his death shall become the statutory tenant and shall remain so as long as he occupies the dwelling-house as his residence. Where there is more than one person so qualified, the statutory tenant shall be the person decided by agreement or in default of agreement by the County Court.

Whether the original tenant's spouse or a member of his family succeeds, the successor must be one person only. For the purpose of succession, 'family' has been interpreted widely to include, in addition to the obvious cases, illegitimate and adopted children, step-children, grand-children and brothers- and sisters-in-law, the common law husband or wife and cousins and nieces — but the latter two only where justified by the particular circumstances.

On the death of the first successor, there are similar pro-

visions for a second succession but not for further successions.
A statutory tenancy may be determined by the tenant giving
up possession or by his having an order for possession made
against him. A statutory tenancy may cease to exist where
the tenant no longer occupies the dwelling-house as his residence or where the dwelling-house is destroyed by fire.

8.2.4   Regulated tenancies

A regulated tenancy may be a protected tenancy or a statutory
tenancy (including in the latter case a first or second succession) unless it has been released from the provisions of the
1977 Act by an order made by the Secretary of State. A
tenancy is not a regulated tenancy if it is a tenancy to which
Part II of the *Landlord and Tenant Act 1954* applies.

Rent limits may vary according to whether the regulated
tenancy is in a contractual or a statutory period and to
whether there is a registered rent.

Where during a contractual period of a regulated tenancy
a rent is registered (see below), the rent recoverable shall be
limited to that rent and where the rent agreed between the
parties exceeds that figure, the excess is irrecoverable: should
the rent registered be greater than the rent agreed between
the parties it will not be possible to recover any sum above
the rent agreed prior to the expiration of the contractual
period. Where a property is let on a protected tenancy there
is no rent limit although it is open to either party to apply
for a fair rent to be registered.

Where there is a registered rent, the rent may be increased
by a notice specifying a date not more than four weeks prior
to the date of the notice and not earlier than the date of
registration. Subject to this proviso, the date of registration
may be specified as the date for the increase, even though
that date falls other than at the beginning of a rental period.

There are provisions for the appointment of Rent Officers
in connection with the fixing of fair rents: the Rent Officer
for the area must maintain a register of rents available for
inspection, a certified copy of any entry therein being available to any person on payment of a prescribed fee. Rent
Assessment Committees operate as appeal bodies.

The fair rent is to be arrived at in accordance with the provisions of section 70 of the *Rent Act 1977* as amended by the *Housing Act 1980*, the thrust of the section being to exclude any part of the rental value attributable to scarcity. In view of its importance, the section is quoted in full:

'(1) In determining, for the purposes of this Part of this Act, what rent is or would be a fair rent under a regulated tenancy of a dwelling-house, regard shall be had to all the circumstances (other than personal circumstances) and in particular to —
   (a) the age, character, locality and state of repair of the dwelling-house, and
   (b) if any furniture is provided for use under the tenancy, the quantity, quality and condition of the furniture.

(2) For the purposes of the determination it shall be assumed that the number of persons seeking to become tenants of similar dwelling-houses in the locality on the terms (other than those relating to rent) of the regulated tenancy is not substantially greater than the number of such dwelling-houses in the locality which are available for letting on such terms.

(3) There shall be disregarded —
   (a) any disrepair or other defect attributable to a failure by the tenant under the regulated tenancy or any predecessor in title of his to comply with any terms thereof:
   (b) any improvement carried out, otherwise than in pursuance of the terms of the tenancy, by the tenant under the regulated tenancy or any predecessor in title of his:
   ((c) and (d) have been repealed)
   (e) if any furniture is provided for use under the regulated tenancy or any predecessor in title of his or, as the case may be, any deterioration in the condition of the furniture due to any ill-treatment by the tenant, any person residing or lodging with him, or any sub-tenant of his.

(4) In this section "improvement" includes the replacement of any fixture or fittings.'

Registered rents may now be reviewed on application every two years but the full effect of any increase is delayed for one year by the phasing provisions of section 60(3) of the *Housing Act 1980*. This section sets out a formula which enables calculation of the new rent limit, the formula being

$$\tfrac{1}{2}(P + S + R)$$

where

    P is the previous rent limit
    S is the service element
    R is the registered rent

The phasing provisions do not apply to any part of the increase attributable to payment for services which is payable in full. An example may be useful.

The Rent Officer has registered a rent of £18 per week including a sum of £4 per week for services in place of the previous rent of £14 which included £3 for services. The rent limit for the first year will be

$$\tfrac{1}{2}(14 + 1 + 18) = £16.50$$

an increase of £2.50 per week, after which the rent will rise to the full registered rent. The earlier rent was £11 exclusive of services and has been increased to £14. Half of this increase together with the new service charge added to the earlier rent is

$$£1.50 + £4 + £11 = £16.50$$

The landlord is entitled to add the weekly equivalent of any rates payments made by him.

Where no rent has been registered, there is no restriction on the rent which may be agreed between the landlord and a *new* tenant. However, the tenant is at liberty at any time to make application to the Rent Officer to fix and register a fair rent.

A tenancy may become a regulated tenancy by conversion: in particular section 64 of the *Housing Act 1980* converted all remaining controlled tenancies into regulated tenancies with one exception. The exception to the conversion of a controlled tenancy into a regulated tenancy is where the tenancy comprises mixed business and residential user, in which case the tenancy becomes subject to Part II of the *Landlord and Tenant Act 1954.*

Where there is a tenancy by conversion, any agreement as to increased rent entered into on or after 28 November 1980 shall be of no effect. Unless the increase is made as a result of a rent fixed by the rent officer, the increase is void and the tenant may recover any excess within one year of payment.

8.2.5 Restricted contracts

A restricted contract is one where one person grants to another in consideration of a rent which includes payment for the use of furniture or for services, the right to occupy a dwelling as a residence. Where the dwelling consists of only part of a house it is a restricted contract if the person has exclusive occupation of part, even though other rooms or accommodation in the house are used in common with any other person or persons.

> By section 19(8), 'services' includes 'attendance, the provision of heating or lighting, the supply of hot water and any other privilege or facility connected with the occupancy of a dwelling, other than a privilege or facility requisite for the purpose of access, cold water supply or sanitary accommodation'

In contrast, there is no statutory definition of 'furniture' though it is clear from decided cases that it must consist of more than one or two items and does not include fixtures and fittings in the dwelling nor furniture in the common parts.

Where a tenancy is precluded from being a protected tenancy solely because it was granted by a resident landlord it shall be a restricted contract notwithstanding that the rent may not include payment for the use of furniture or for services.

A contract is not a restricted contract if

(a) The rateable value of the dwelling on the approximate day exceeded certain specified limits (Classes D and E in Table 8.1)

Table 8.1   Rateable value limits beyond which Rent Acts do not afford protection

Description	Class	Appropriate day	Rateable value exceeding	
			in Greater London	Elsewhere
Protected tenancies	A	on or after 1 April 1973	£1500	£750
	B	on or after 22 March 1973 but before 1 April 1973	600	300
		and on 1 April 1973	1500	750
	C	before 22 March 1973 and	400	200
		on 22 March 1973 and	600	300
		on 1 April 1973	1500	750
Restricted contracts	D	on or after 1 April 1973	1500	750
	E	before 1 April 1973	400	200
		on 1 April 1973	1500	750
Tenancies at low rents		before 22 March 1973	400	200

(b) It creates a regulated tenancy or
(c) Under the contract the interest of the lessor belongs to Her Majesty in right of the Crown or to a government department, or is held in trust for Her Majesty for the purpose of a government department or
(d) It is a contract for the letting of any premises at a rent which includes payment in respect of board the value of which forms a substantial proportion of the whole or
(e) It is a protected occupancy under the *Rent (Agriculture) Act 1976* or
(f) It creates a tenancy granted by a housing association, housing trust or the Housing Corporation

A contractual licence may be a restricted contract where board is not provided. A tenancy which is precluded from being a protected tenancy solely because it was granted by a resident landlord shall be treated as a restricted contract even though there is payment for attendance. Similarly, where a tenant shares certain accommodation with his landlord while enjoying exclusive occupation of other accommodation under a tenancy which does not qualify as a protected tenancy, the tenancy is a restricted contract. Both provisions apply notwithstanding that no payment for the use of furniture or for services is included in the rent. The Secretary of State may by order exclude from these provisions any dwelling where the rateable value exceeds such amount as may be specified: the order may apply generally or only to certain types of dwellings and certain areas of England and Wales.

Arrangements for the review of rents and for their phasing are similar to those described for regulated rents under registered tenancies, though the procedure is different.

8.2.6 Protected shorthold tenancies

The Act introduces a new type of tenancy to be known as a protected shorthold tenancy.

The purpose is to allow landlords to let for a fixed term of between one and five years with an assurance of possession at the end of the period.

Tenants enjoy the rent control provisions which apply to

regulated tenancies but have no security of tenure at the end of the term.

A protected shorthold tenancy must satisfy the following conditions

(a) It is granted after 28 November 1980
(b) It is granted for a term certain of not less than one and not more than five years and cannot be terminated by the landlord earlier than the expiry of the term except in pursuance of a provision for re-entry or forfeiture for non-payment of rent or breach of any other obligation under the tenancy
(c) Before the grant the landlord has given the tenant a valid notice (to comply with regulations made by the Secretary of State) stating that the tenancy is to be a protected shorthold tenancy
(d) Either there is a regulated rent when the tenancy is granted or a certificate of fair rent has been issued before the grant and the rent payable for any period before a rent is registered does not exceed the rent specified in the certificate and an application is made within 28 days of the beginning of the term and is not withdrawn
(e) The tenant was not a protected or statutory tenant of the dwelling house immediately before the tenancy was granted
(f) It qualifies in all other respects as a protected tenancy

Although the tenancy is granted for a term certain, the tenant may terminate the tenancy before the end of the term by giving one month's notice where the original term is two years or less and three months otherwise.

8.2.7 Other forms of tenancy: assured tenancies

In an endeavour to encourage investors to build houses to let, the Government introduced provisions in the *Housing Act 1980* to enable certain approved bodies to let outside the provisions of the Rent Acts but subject to those provisions for renewal of lease and obtaining possession contained in Part II of the *Landlord and Tenant Act 1954* and which have hitherto worked well in relation to business premises.

To qualify, construction must have commenced after 8 August 1980 and prior to the tenant's occupation, no part let other than under an assured tenancy.

8.2.8 Secure tenancies

Secure tenancies are public sector tenancies and are therefore not considered further.

8.3 GROUNDS FOR POSSESSION

There are now nineteen grounds — termed cases — for possession of dwelling-houses let on or subject to protected or statutory tenancies, the first nine of which are discretionary.

8.3.1 Discretionary cases (1 to 10)

The court may order possession under

Case 1

'Where any rent lawfully due from the tenant has not been paid, or any obligation of the protected or statutory tenancy which arises under this Act, or —

(a) in the case of a protected tenancy, any other obligation of the tenancy, in so far as is consistent with the provisions of Part VII of this Act, or

(b) in the case of a statutory tenancy, any other obligation of the previous protected tenancy which is applicable to the statutory tenancy,

has been broken or not performed.'

The rent must be lawfully due and unpaid at the date of the commencement of proceedings. Payment of arrears into court after this date will not remove the case from the jurisdiction of the court although it is then less likely to be reasonable to make the order. In any event, the order is likely to be made suspended so long as the rent is paid together with a specified amount off the arrears.

'Any obligation' is wide enough to embrace breaches of implied covenants.

Case 2

'Where the tenant or any person residing or lodging with him or any sub-tenant of his has been guilty of conduct which is a nuisance or annoyance to adjoining occupiers, or has been convicted of using the dwelling-house or allowing the dwelling-house to be used for immoral or illegal purposes.'

Nuisance or annoyance together extend to a wide range of possibilities.

Some helpful comments on the second ground of this Case were made by Widgery L. J. in Abrahams *v.* Wilson 1971 —

'If the drugs are on the demised premises merely because the tenant is there and has them in his or her immediate custody . . . then I would say without hesitation that that does not involve a "using" of the premises in connection with the offence. On the other hand, if the premises are employed as a storage place or hiding place for dangerous drugs, a conviction for possession of such drugs, when the conviction is illuminated by further evidence to show the manner in which the drugs themselves were located, would I think be sufficient to satisfy the section and come within case 2.'

Case 3

'Where the condition of the dwelling-house has, in the opinion of the court, deteriorated owing to acts of waste by, or the neglect or default of, the tenant or any person residing or lodging with him or any sub-tenant of his and, in the case of any act of waste by, or the neglect or default of, a person lodging with the tenant or a sub-tenant of his, where the court is satisfied that the tenant has not, before the making of the order in question, taken such steps as he ought reasonably to have taken for the removal of the lodger or sub-tenant, as the case may be.'

This is a widely drawn ground enabling the landlord to obtain a remedy where the property is suffering deterioration.

Case 4

'Where the condition of any furniture provided for use

under the tenancy has, in the opinion of the court, deteriorated owing to ill-treatment by the tenant or any person residing or lodging with him or any sub-tenant of his and, in the case of any ill-treatment by a person lodging with the tenant or a sub-tenant of his, where the court is satisfied that the tenant has not, before the making of the order in question, taken such steps as he ought reasonably to have taken for the removal of the lodger or sub-tenant, as the case may be.'

Cases 3 and 4 may be seen together and reflect the common law obligations of a tenant to behave in a tenant-like fashion.

Case 5

'Where the tenant has given notice to quit and, in consequence of that notice, the landlord has contracted to sell or let the dwelling-house or has taken any other steps as the result of which he would, in the opinion of the court, be seriously prejudiced if he could not obtain possession.'

There must be a valid notice to quit (as to which see page 134 above).

The term 'seriously prejudiced' suggests that the landlord had committed himself contractually for the sale or letting of the premises. Perhaps it would extend to a case where the landlord had committed himself to expenditure in anticipation of selling the property with vacant possession.

Case 6

This is dealt with under paragraph 8.11, tied accommodation.

This case applies even though the contractual tenancy contains no covenant prohibiting assignment and sub-letting. A statutory tenant has no power of assignment.

Case 7

This case applied to controlled tenancies which were converted by section 64 of the *Housing Act*. In general such tenancies became regulated tenancies but where the premises were let partly as a dwelling-house and partly for business purposes the tenancy now proceeds under Part II of the *Landlord and Tenant Act 1954*.

Case 8

'Where the dwelling-house is reasonably required by the landlord for occupation as a residence for some person engaged in his whole-time employment, or in the whole-time employment of some tenant from him or with whom, conditional on housing being provided, a contract for such employment has been entered into, and the tenant was in the employment of the landlord or a former landlord, and the dwelling-house was let to him in consequence of that employment and he has ceased to be in that employment.'

The court may order payment of compensation where it appears to the court that an order for possession was obtained by misrepresentation or concealment of material facts. The amount of compensation is to be ' . . . such sum as appears sufficient as compensation for damage or loss sustained by that tenant as a result of the order.'

There are separate provisions relating to dwelling houses occupied by agricultural workers (see cases 16 to 18 and separate note 8.12).

Case 9

'Where the dwelling-house is reasonably required by the landlord for occupation as a residence for —

(a)   himself, or
(b)   any son or daughter of his over 18 years of age, or
(c)   his father or mother, or
(d)   if the dwelling-house is let on or subject to a regulated tenancy, the father or mother of his wife or husband.

and the landlord did not become landlord by purchasing the dwelling-house or any interest therein after —

(i)   7th November 1956, in the case of a tenancy which was then a controlled tenancy;
(ii)   8th March 1973, in the case of a tenancy which became a regulated tenancy by virtue of section 14 of the Counter-Inflation Act 1973;
(iii)   24th May 1974, in the case of a regulated furnished tenancy; or
(iv)   23rd March 1965, in the case of any other tenancy.'

Schedule 15 provides in Part III

'1. A court shall not make an order for possession of a dwelling-house by reason only that the circumstances of the case fall within Case 9 in Part I of this Schedule if the court is satisfied that, having regard to all the circumstances of the case, including the question whether other accommodation is available for the landlord or the tenant, greater hardship would be caused by granting the order than by refusing to grant it.'

As will be seen, the parties for whom the dwelling-house may be required are limited and the relationships are more restricted than those in the case of statutory succession. Where the dwelling-house was purchased with vacant possession the provisions restricting use of this case do not apply: the reference is specifically to becoming a *landlord* by purchase.

Case 10

'Where the court is satisfied that the rent charged by the tenant —

(a) for any sublet part of the dwelling-house which is a dwelling-house let on a protected tenancy or subject to a statutory tenancy is or was in excess of the maximum rent for the time being recoverable for that part, having regard to Part III of this Act, or

(b) for any sublet part of the dwelling-house which is subject to a restricted contract is or was in excess of the maximum (if any) which it is lawful for the lessor, within the meaning of Part V of this Act to require or receive having regard to the provisions of that Part.'

8.3.2 Mandatory cases (11 to 20)

The mandatory grounds for possession are set out below. In particular it is necessary that not later than the relevant date the landlord gave notice in writing to the tenant that possession might be recovered under the specified case. The 'relevant date' for mandatory cases is the date of commencement of the regulated tenancy except where

(a) A tenancy became a regulated tenancy by virtue of section 73 of the *Housing Act 1980* (dwellings forming part of Crown Estates or belonging to Duchies) in which case the relevant date is 8 February 1981 or

(b) A regulated furnished tenancy was created before 14 August 1974 when the relevant date is 13 February 1975 or

(c) A tenancy created before 22 March 1973 became a regulated tenancy by virtue of the *Counter-Inflation Act 1973* when the relevant date is 22 September 1973 or

(d) A protected tenancy was created before 8 December 1965 when the relevant date is 7 June 1966

Case 11

'Where a person who occupied the dwelling-house as his residence (in this Case referred to as "the owner-occupier") let it on a regulated tenancy and —

(a) not later than the relevant date the landlord gave notice in writing to the tenant that possession might be recovered under this Case, and

(b) the dwelling-house has not, since —

(i) 22nd March 1973, in the case of a tenancy which became a regulated tenancy by virtue of section 14 of the Counter-Inflation Act 1973;

(ii) 14th August 1974, in the case of a regulated furnished tenancy; or

(iii) 8th December 1965, in the case of any other tenancy.

been let by the owner-occupier on a protected tenancy with respect to which the condition mentioned in paragraph (a) above was not satisfied, and

(c) the court is of the opinion that of the conditions set out in Part V of this Schedule one of those in paragraphs (a) and (c) to (f) is satisfied.'

The court has discretion to dispense with the requirements of either or both paragraphs (a) and (b) where it is of the opinion that it is just and equitable to do so.

Part V of the Schedule referred to in (c) above and in Case 12 following was introduced by the *Housing Act 1980* and provides —

'2. The conditions referred to in paragraph (c) in each of Cases 11 and 12 are that —

(a) the dwelling-house is required as a residence for the owner or any member of his family who resided with the owner when he last occupied the dwelling-house as a residence;

(b) the owner has retired from regular employment and requires the dwelling-house as a residence;

(c) the owner has died and the dwelling-house is required as a residence for a member of his family who was residing with him at the time of his death;

(d) the owner has died and the dwelling-house is required by a successor in title as his residence or for the purpose of disposing of it with vacant possession;

(e) the dwelling-house is subject to a mortgage, made by deed and granted before the tenancy, and the mortgagee —

(i) is entitled to exercise a power of sale conferred on him by the mortgage or by section 101 of the Law of Property Act 1925; and

(ii) requires the dwelling-house for the purpose of disposing of it with vacant possession in exercise of that power; and

(f) the dwelling-house is not reasonably suitable to the needs of the owner, having regard to his place of work, and he requires it for the purpose of disposing of it with vacant possession and of using the proceeds of that disposal in acquiring, as his residence, a dwelling-house which is more suitable to those needs.'

It has been held that Case 11 permits of a wider interpretation than Case 9 in that the former case does not qualify 'require' by the word 'reasonably': all that is necessary is that the landlord has a genuine and *bona fide* intention.

Case 12

'Where the landlord (in this Case referred to as 'the owner') intends to occupy the dwelling-house as his residence at such time as he might retire from regular employment and has let it on a regulated tenancy before he has so retired and —

(a)   not later than the relevant date the landlord gave notice in writing to the tenant that possession might be recovered under this Case; and

(b)   the dwelling-house has not, since 14th August 1974, been let by the owner on a protected tenancy with respect to which the condition mentioned in paragraph (a) above was not satisfied; and

(c)   the court is of the opinion that of the conditions set out in Part V of this Schedule (reproduced above) one of those conditions in paragraphs (b) to (e) is satisfied.

If the court is of the opinion that, notwithstanding that the condition in paragraph (a) or (b) above is not complied with, it is just and equitable to make an order for possession of the dwelling-house, the court may dispense with the requirements of either or both of those paragraphs, as the case may require.'

The practical effect of this case is to allow purchase and letting of premises intended for occupation in retirement: the case is of importance in particular to occupiers of 'tied' accommodation who wish to acquire a home some time before it will be required and to obtain an income from it in the meanwhile.

Case 13

'Where the dwelling-house is let under a tenancy for a term of years certain not exceeding 8 months and —

(a)   not later than the relevant date the landlord gave notice in writing to the tenant that possession might be recovered under this Case; and

(b)   the dwelling-house was, at some time within the period of 12 months ending on the relevant date, occupied under a right to occupy it for a holiday.

For the purposes of this Case a tenancy shall be treated as being for a term of years certain notwithstanding that it is liable to determination by re-entry or on the happening of any event other than the giving of notice by the landlord to determine the term.'

This case is intended to cover out of season lettings of holiday homes where the dwelling-house had been occupied (not necessarily let) for a holiday within a previous specified period.

Case 14

'Where the dwelling-house is let under a tenancy for a term of years certain not exceeding 12 months and —

(a) not later than the relevant date the landlord gave notice in writing to the tenant that possession might be recovered under this Case; and

(b) at some time within the period of 12 months ending on the relevant date, the dwelling-house was subject to such a tenancy as is referred to in section 8(1) of this Act.

For the purposes of this Case a tenancy shall be treated as being for a term of years certain notwithstanding that it is liable to determination by re-entry or on the happening of any event other than the giving of notice by the landlord to determine the term.'

This case refers to 'vacation lettings' and enables specified educational institutions to let accommodation for short periods to non-students without granting security of tenure.

Case 15

'Where the dwelling-house is held for the purpose of being available for occupation by a minister of religion as a residence from which to perform the duties of his office and —

(a) not later than the relevant date the tenant was given notice in writing that possession might be recovered under this Case, and

(b) the court is satisfied that the dwelling-house is

required for occupation by a minister of religion as such a residence.'

Case 16

'Where the dwelling-house was at any time occupied by a person under the terms of his employment as a person employed in agriculture, and

(a) the tenant neither is nor at any time was so employed by the landlord and is not the widow of a person who was so employed, and

(b) not later than the relevant date, the tenant was given notice in writing that possession might be recovered under this Case, and

(c) the court is satisfied that the dwelling-house is required for occupation by a person employed, or to be employed, by the landlord in agriculture.

For the purposes of this Case "employed", "employment" and "agriculture" have the same meanings as in the Agricultural Wages Act 1948.'

Case 17

'Where proposals for amalgamation, approved for the purposes of a scheme under section 26 of the Agriculture Act 1967, have been carried out and, at the time when the proposals were submitted, the dwelling-house was occupied by a person responsible (whether as owner, tenant, or servant or agent of another) for the control of the farming of any part of the land comprised in the amalgamation and

(a) after the carrying out of the proposals, the dwelling-house was let on a regulated tenancy otherwise than to, or to the widow of, either a person ceasing to be so responsible as part of the amalgamation or a person who is, or at any time was, employed by the landlord in agriculture, and

(b) not later than the relevant date the tenant was given notice in writing that possession might be recovered under this Case, and

(c) the court is satisfied that the dwelling-house is

required for occupation by a person employed, or to
be employed, by the landlord in agriculture, and
(d) the proceedings for possession are commenced by the
landlord at any time during the period of 5 years
beginning with the date on which the proposals for
the amalgamation were approved or, if occupation of
the dwelling-house after the amalgamation continued in, or was first taken by, a person ceasing
to be responsible as mentioned in paragraph (a)
above or his widow, during a period expiring 3 years
after the date on which the dwelling-house next
became unoccupied.
For the purposes of this Case "employed" and "agriculture" have the same meanings as in the Agricultural
Wages Act 1948 and "amalgamation" has the same meaning
as in Part II of the Agriculture Act 1967.'

Case 18
'Where —
(a) the last occupier of the dwelling-house before the
relevant date was a person, or the widow of a person,
who was at some time during his occupation responsible (whether as owner, tenant, or servant or
agent of another) for the control of the farming land
which formed, together with the dwelling-house, an
agricultural unit within the meaning of the Agriculture
Act 1947, and
(b) the tenant is neither —

(i)   a person, or the widow of a person, who is or
has at any time been responsible for the control
of the farming of any part of the said land, nor
(ii) a person, or the widow of a person, who is or at
any time was employed by the landlord in
agriculture, and

(c) the creation of the tenancy was not preceded by the
carrying out in connection with any of the said land
of an amalgamation approved for the purposes of a
scheme under section 26 of the Agriculture Act 1967,
and
(d) not later than the relevant date the tenant was given

notice in writing that possession might be recovered under this Case, and

(e) the court is satisfied that the dwelling-house is required for occupation either by a person responsible or to be responsible (whether as owner, tenant, or servant or agent of another) for the control of the farming of any part of the said land or by a person employed or to be employed by the landlord in agriculture, and

(f) in a case where the relevant date was before 9th August 1972, the proceedings for possession are commenced by the landlord before the expiry of 5 years from the date on which the occupier referred to in paragraph (a) above went out of occupation.

For the purposes of this Case "employed" and "agriculture" have the same meanings as in the Agricultural Wages Act 1948 and "amalgamation" has the same meaning as in Part II of the Agriculture Act 1967.'

Case 19

'Where the dwelling-house was let under a protected shorthold tenancy (or is treated under section 55 of the Housing Act 1980 as having been so let) and —

(a) there either has been no grant of a further tenancy of the dwelling-house since the end of the protected shorthold tenancy or, if there was such a grant, it was to a person who immediately before the grant was in possession of the dwelling-house as a protected or statutory tenant; and

(b) the proceedings for possession were commenced after appropriate notice by the landlord to the tenant and not later than 3 months after the expiry of the notice.

A notice is appropriate for this Case if —

(i) it is in writing and states that proceedings for possession under this Case may be brought after its expiry; and

(ii) it expires not earlier than 3 months after it is served nor, if, when it is served, the tenancy is a periodic

tenancy, before that periodic tenancy could be brought to an end by a notice to quit served by the landlord on the same day;
(iii) it is served —
    (a) in the period of three months immediately preceding the date on which the protected shorthold tenancy comes to an end; or
    (b) if that date has passed, in the period of three months immediately preceding any anniversary of that date; and
(iv) in a case where a previous notice has been served by the landlord on the tenant in respect of the dwelling-house, and that notice was an appropriate notice, it is served not earlier than 3 months after the expiry of the previous notice.

A relaxation of these provisions is introduced by section 55(2) of the *Housing Act 1980* which provides —

'If, in proceedings for possession under Case 19 set out above, the court is of opinion that, notwithstanding that the condition of paragraph (b) or (c) of section 52(1) above is not satisfied, it is just and equitable to make an order for possession, it may treat the tenancy under which the dwelling-house was let as a protected shorthold tenancy'

Case 20

'Where the dwelling-house was let by a person (in this Case referred to as "the owner") at any time after the commencement of section 67 of the Housing Act 1980 (28 November 1980)

(a) at the time when the owner acquired the dwelling-house he was a member of the regular armed forces of the Crown;
(b) at the relevant date the owner was a member of the regular armed forces of the Crown;
(c) not later than the relevant date the owner gave notice in writing to the tenant that possession might be recovered under this Case;
(d) the dwelling-house has not, since the commencement of section 67 of the Act of 1980 been let by the

owner on a protected tenancy with respect to which the condition mentioned in paragraph (c) above was not satisfied; and

(e)   the court is of the opinion that —
  (i) the dwelling-house is required as a residence for the owner; or
  (ii) of the conditions set out in Part V of this Schedule one of those in paragraphs (c) to (f) is satisfied.

If the court is of the opinion that, notwithstanding that the condition in paragraph (c) or (d) above is not complied with, it is just and equitable to make an order for possession of the dwelling-house, the court may dispense with the requirements of either or both of these paragraphs, as the case may require.

For the purposes of this Case "regular armed forces of the Crown" has the same meaning as in section 1 of the House of Commons Disqualification Act 1975.'

Other amendments to the law relating to security of tenure were introduced by the *Housing Act 1980*.

8.4   RESTRICTED CONTRACTS

Where a contract has been entered into since 28 November 1980 (the date of commencement of section 69) it is provided that on the making of an order for possession or at any time up to its execution, the court may either stay or suspend execution of the order or postpone the date of possession for such period as it thinks fit but not later than three months after the making of the order. When acting in this way the court shall impose conditions including as to the payment of arrears (if any) and mesne profits for the period of occupation after termination of the tenancy unless it considers that it would cause exceptional hardship to the lessee or would otherwise be unreasonable.

8.5   SUB-LETTINGS

The protection afforded to a tenant is personal to him and will be lost unless the tenant is in possession of at least part of the premises and that part is protected under the Acts.

Occupation is an essential element in the status of a statutory tenant.

Section 23 of the *Rent Act 1977* provides that a tenant shall not lose protection solely because a sub-letting of any part of the premises includes the sharing of accommodation or the provision of board or attendance.

Where a court makes an order for possession against a protected or statutory tenant under one of the cases in the 1977 Act the order does not extend to a sub-tenant to whom the dwelling-house or any part of it had been lawfully sublet before the commencement of proceedings for possession. The sub-tenant becomes the tenant of the landlord on the same terms as previously enjoyed by the tenant: where only part of the premises is occupied by the sub-tenant the rent payable under the superior tenancy is to be apportioned.

Where the sub-tenancy includes provision by the immediate landlord of furniture or services the superior landlord has an opportunity to avoid such parts of the agreement by notice within six weeks of the termination of the statutorily protected tenancy.

The tenant is required to give to his landlord details of any sub-letting, including the rent charged, within 14 days of the sub-letting, except where the terms are the same as a previously notified sub-letting of that part. Sub-letting itself offers two discretionary grounds on which the court may grant possession:

(a) Case 6 where, without the consent of the landlord, the tenant has assigned or sub-let the whole of the dwelling-house or sub-let part of the dwelling-house, the remainder being already sub-let

(b) Case 10 where the court is satisfied that the rent charged by the tenant for any sub-let part of the dwelling-house is in excess of the maximum rent for the time being recoverable for that part

Finally, in respect of assured tenancies the landlord may oppose a new tenancy on what may be termed economic grounds, where the current tenancy was created by the sub-letting of part only of the property and the landlord can show that the aggregate of the rents reasonably obtainable on separate lettings would in total be substantially less than

the rent reasonably obtainable on a letting of that property
as a whole.

The *Matrimonial Homes Act 1967* makes detailed provisions for the non-tenant spouse in occupation of the
dwelling-house to be protected from eviction and where not
in occupation a right with leave of the court to enter and
occupy. Possession by the non-tenant spouse is to be treated
as possession by the tenant spouse, all as long as the marriage
subsists. There are further provisions whereby the court is
empowered to order that as regards parties to divorce proceedings then from the date of the decree absolute, one
party shall cease to be entitled to occupy the dwelling-house
and the other party shall be deemed to be the tenant or the
sole tenant under the protected or statutory tenancy.

8.6   PREMIUMS

For the purposes of the Rent Acts a premium is defined as
including

'(a)   any fine or other like sum;
(b)   any other pecuniary consideration in addition to rent;
      and
(c)   any sum paid by way of a deposit, other than one
      which does not exceed one-sixth of the annual rent
      and is reasonable in relation to the potential liability
      in respect of which it is paid.'

Section 120 of the *Rent Act 1977* makes it unlawful to
require or to accept a premium, as defined above, as a condition of the grant, renewal or continuance of a protected
tenancy. In addition to imposing a fine, the court may order
the amount of the premium to be repaid.

Similar provisions are made in relation to payments required
as a condition of the grant, renewal, continuance or assignment of rights under a restricted contract. There are exceptions
where payment is for a proper proportion of outgoings or
where a reasonable amount is paid in respect of goodwill of
a business, trade or profession.

Where the purchase of any furniture is required as a
condition of the grant, renewal, continuance or assignment
of a protected tenancy or the rights under a restricted con-

tract the amount, if any, by which the amount exceeds a reasonable price for the furniture shall be treated as if it were a premium.

Where a regulated tenancy is to be granted, continued or renewed any requirement that rent shall be payable before the beginning of the rental period or earlier than six months before the end of the rental period where that period is more than six months, shall be void and the rent irrecoverable. Where such payments have been made they may be recovered for up to two years after payment by deduction from rent or from the landlord or his personal representatives. These payments are regarded as rent in advance and avoidable in the circumstances given. Additionally, illegal premiums paid may be recovered from the person to whom they were paid (not necessarily the landlord).

There are separate provisions in respect of premiums in relation to certain long tenancies.

8.7   SERVICE CHARGES

The provision of services by the landlord, reimbursed by the payment of a service charge by the tenant or tenants, is an area which has been subject to some form of control. The provisions were not always satisfactory or sufficiently comprehensive and new rules have been introduced by the *Housing Act 1980*.

The present position is summarized in Section 9.4.

8.8   RENT BOOKS

The *Landlord and Tenant Act 1962* requires rent books to be issued in certain cases, providing in section 1

'(1)   where a person (hereafter in this Act referred to as the "tenant") has a right granted to him or any predecessor in title of his by a contract or conferred by an enactment to occupy any premises as a residence in consideration of a rent, and that rent is payable weekly, it shall be the duty of the landlord to provide a rent book or other similar document for use in respect of the premises.

(2) The foregoing subsection shall not apply to any premises if the rent includes a payment in respect of board and the value of that board to the tenant forms a substantial proportion of the whole rent.'

The Act requires the name and address of the landlord to be given on the rent book and empowers the Department of the Environment to require other information in certain cases with penalties for failing to do so: penalties are also prescribed for failure to give information about rent allowances as required by the *Housing Finance Act 1972*. Several forms are prescribed in the *Rent Book (Forms of Notice) Regulations 1976* (SI 378/1976) for use with tenancies within the *Rent Act 1977*, the one most used being that relating to regulated tenancies which is set out below.

Rent book for Regulated Tenancy

Form of notice to be included in every rent book or other similar document used in connection with a regulated tenancy under which the rent is payable weekly.

INFORMATION FOR TENANT

1. Address of premises..
2. Name and address of landlord ....
3. Name and address of agent (if any) ....
4. The rent inclusive/exclusive of rates is £... per week if a fair rent is registered, paragraph 5 and, where it applies, paragraph 7 must be filled in.
5. The registered rent (which excludes rates) is £... per week. The word 'variable' should be added after the amount of registered rent if the entry in the register permits the landlord to vary the rent, in accordance with the cost of providing services or maintaining or repairing the premises in accordance with the terms shown in the register, without having to have a new rent registered.
6. As a result of the provisions for phasing rent increases following the registration of a fair rent, the maximum rent (exclusive of rates) which the landlord may for the time being charge may be less than the registered rent.
7. In addition to the registered rent £... per week is payable by way of rates borne by the landlord or a superior landlord.

IF A RENT HAS NOT BEEN REGISTERED

8. You or your landlord or both of you acting together may at any time apply to the Rent Officer to have a fair rent registered for the

premises. Your local authority may also apply to the Rent Officer, but only to have a reduced rent registered.

9. Where no rent has been registered and your contractual term has ended then, except in the case where you enter into the new agreement referred to in paragraph 10 below, only limited increases in the rent are permitted, for example for rates increases or improvements (but see paragraph 11 below).

10. You and your landlord may agree to increase the rent under the existing contractual tenancy or to enter into a new tenancy agreement at an increased rent. Any such agreement must be in writing and signed by both you and the landlord, and must contain a statement at the head of the agreement, in conspicuous characters, to the effect that:

(i) your security of tenure will not be affected if you refuse to enter into the agreement, and

(ii) entry into the agreement will not deprive you or the landlord of the right to apply at any time to the Rent Officer for the registration of a fair rent.

11. There are special provisions where grant-aided improvement works have been carried out, and where a tenancy, including a statutory tenancy has been converted from rent control. Your local authority, a Housing Aid Centre or a Citizens' Advice Bureau can give you further information and tell you the address of the Rent Officer.

IF A RENT HAS BEEN REGISTERED

12. The landlord may not charge more rent (exclusive of rates) than is shown in the register, or if an increase of rent must be phased, more than is permitted under the relevant phasing provisions. He may add to this the amount of the rates that he pays for the premises if there is a note on the register that he pays the rates (see paragraph 7 above). In certain cases the registered rent may vary in accordance with the cost of providing services or maintaining or repairing the premises, but only if there is a note on the register to this effect (see paragraph 5 above).

13. The registered rent cannot be changed without applying to the Rent Officer. He will not register a new rent applying within the two years after a registration takes effect, unless an application is made by you and the landlord acting together, or there has been a change in the circumstances taken into account when the rent was registered — for example a change in the terms of the tenancy or the furniture supplied, or in the condition of the premises.

14. Further information on rents of regulated tenancies is set out in a booklet available free of charge at rent offices, Housing Aid Centres, Citizens' Advice Bureaux and local Council Offices.

SUB-LETTING

15. If you sub-let part of the premises and you are not permitted to

do this under your tenancy agreement, your landlord may apply to the county court for an order to evict you.

16. If you sub-let part of the premises, then: —

   (a) if the sub-tenancy is protected under the Rent Act 1968 you must give the landlord, within 14 days, a statement in writing of the sub-letting, giving particulars of occupancy, including the rent charged. The penalty for failing to do this without reasonable excuse, or for giving false particulars, is a fine not exceeding £10. When you have once given the landlord the particulars, you need not do so again if the only change is a change of sub-tenant; and

   (b) if you overcharge your sub-tenant, the landlord may apply to the county court for an order to evict you.

SECURITY OF TENURE

17. If you have a contractual tenancy the landlord must first bring it to an end before he can exercise any of his other rights. If he does so by means of a notice to quit, he must give you at least four weeks' notice in writing and that notice must contain certain prescribed information about tenants' rights.

18. Even after your contractual term ends, your landlord cannot evict you without a court order, which except in certain special cases will be granted only if the court thinks it reasonable to do so and either there is suitable accommodation for you to go to or one of a limited number of conditions is satisfied (for example, you have failed to pay rent, or you or your family have been a nuisance or annoyance to neighbours).

19. It is a criminal offence for your landlord or anyone else to try to make you leave by using force, by harassing you or your family, or by interfering with your home or your possessions unless authorised by the court. If anyone does this, you should complain to your local authority.

RENT ALLOWANCES

20. If you have difficulty in paying your rent you may apply to your local authority for a rent allowance. When the rent is payable weekly, the landlord is obliged to insert in this rent book appropriate particulars of your local authority's rent allowance scheme. You may obtain further details of the scheme, and also details of your local authority's rate rebate scheme, from your local Council Offices.

8.9   EVICTION

A court may make an order for possession which must normally take effect not later than 14 days after the making of the order: where the court considers that exceptional hardship would be the result of such an order the period may be extended but not in any event to a date later than six weeks after the making of the order.

These restrictions on the exercise of the discretion of the court do not apply if

(a) The order is made in an action by a mortgagee for possession or
(b) The order is made in an action for forfeiture of a lease or
(c) The court had power to make the order only if it considered it reasonable to do so (refers to an order for possession in respect of a dwelling-house let on a protected tenancy or subject to a statutory tenancy) or
(d) The order relates to a dwelling-house which is the subject of a restricted contract or
(e) The order is made in proceedings for possession of a dwelling-house which is being acquired by the occupier on a 'rental—purchase' basis

It should be noted that for the purposes of Part I of the *Protection from Eviction Act 1977* a person who, under the terms of his employment, had exclusive possession of any premises other than as a tenant shall be deemed to have been a tenant.

There is now an exception to these provisions in respect of protected shorthold tenancies. Where the landlord becomes entitled, as against the tenant, to possession of the dwelling-house, he shall also be entitled to possession against the sub-tenant. This provision commences with the grant of the shorthold and continues until either no person is in possession as a protected or statutory tenant, or a protected tenancy is granted to a person who was not, immediately before the grant, in possession of the dwelling-house as a protected or statutory tenant.

8.9.1 Protection from eviction

The law on eviction from dwelling-houses has been consolidated in the *Protection from Eviction Act 1977* as amended by the *Housing Act 1980*.

8.9.2   Unlawful eviction and harassment

The Act is concerned with unlawful eviction and harassment of the residential occupier, whether he occupies under a contract or by virtue of any enactment or rule of law allowing him to remain in possession or restricting the right of any other person to recover possession.

Any person who unlawfully deprives or attempts to deprive the occupier of his occupation or does acts calculated to interfere with his peace or comfort or persistently withdraws or withholds services reasonably required with intent to cause him to give up occupation or to refrain from exercising any right in respect of the premises or part thereof shall be guilty of a criminal offence for which penalties are laid down. There may also be a claim in civil proceedings.

8.9.3   Restriction on re-entry

Where the premises are let on a lease subject to a right of re-entry or forfeiture there must nevertheless be proceedings in court to enforce the right while any person is lawfully residing on the premises or part of them. This section is specifically provided to be binding on the Crown.

8.9.4   Eviction only by due process of law

The owner may not enforce against the occupier his right to recover possession of the premises where a tenancy which is not a statutorily protected tenancy comes to an end, otherwise than by proceedings in the court. This provision also applies where the owner's right to recover possession arises on the death of the tenant under a statutory tenancy.

8.9.5   Validity of notices to quit

No notice to quit by a landlord or a tenant shall be valid unless it is in writing, contains prescribed information and is given not less than four weeks before the date on which it is to take effect. The form of notices to quit has been discussed earlier (Section 8.4).

8.10   DISTRESS

Distress is the process whereby a landlord, either personally or through a bailiff, seizes goods belonging to the tenant in order to raise sufficient money on sale to discharge arrears of rent. So far as protected and statutory tenancies are concerned, no distress shall be levied except by leave of the County Court which has discretionary powers to adjourn proceedings or to stay, suspend or postpone any order. These provisions do not apply to restricted contracts. Where the distress is levied under section 137 of the *County Courts Act 1959* the landlord is given some priority over other creditors.

8.11   TIED ACCOMMODATION

A landlord—tenant relationship may arise by virtue of the fact that the occupier of the dwelling-house is employed by the owner. The occupier may be in possession by virtue of a tenancy agreement or of a licence: the accommodation may or may not be essential to the proper execution of his employment.

The precise facts of occupation will determine the extent and form of the protection available.

Where there is a service tenancy (as opposed to a licence) the Rent Acts will apply in which case there is a discretionary ground for possession available to the landlord —

Case 8

'Where the dwelling-house is reasonably required by the landlord for occupation as a residence for some person engaged in his wholetime employment, or in the wholetime employment of some tenant from him or with whom, conditional on housing being provided, a contract for such employment has been entered into, and the tenant was in the employment of the landlord or a former landlord, and the dwelling-house was let to him in consequence of that employment and he has ceased to be in that employment.'

Where occupation is not within the provisions of the Rent Acts, it is nevertheless provided that any person who, under the terms of his employment, had exclusive possession of any premises other than as a tenant shall be deemed to have been

a tenant in relation to the procedures for regaining possession
by the landlord.

8.12   PROTECTION FOR AGRICULTURAL WORKERS

The provisions of the *Rent (Agriculture) Act 1976* (as
amended by the *Housing Act 1980*) are intended to protect
agricultural workers occupying dwelling houses either as
tenants or as licensees.

Special provisions are necessary in relation to houses
occupied by agricultural workers because they would only
rarely be protected by the Rent Acts. For example, many
houses are occupied rent free or at a nominal rent: sometimes
some meals are provided also. Occupation comes about contractually and is referred to as a protected occupancy: the
Act does not come into operation unless and until the contract is terminated, when it is converted into a statutory
tenancy (but of a type created especially for the purposes of
the Act and not to be confused with a statutory tenancy
under the Rent Acts).

Where the tenancy qualifies under the Rent Acts the tenant
is entitled to the protection afforded by those Acts. The rights
of the statutory tenant under the 1976 Act are akin to those
provided by the Rent Acts although some matters of detail
differ: principally the grounds on which possession may be
ordered, succession limited to one occasion and protection
where the accommodation is shared with anyone other than
the landlord or the employer.

The terms of the new statutory tenancy are implied by the
Act. They include a provision that the rent payable must not
exceed the registered rent if there is one or otherwise an
amount not exceeding one and a half times the rateable
value. The rent is fixed either by agreement between the
parties or following the service of a section 12 notice by the
landlord setting out the basis of the rent and is a provisional
rent pending application to the Rent Officer for registration.
The tenant will be liable to pay rates or to reimburse his
landlord once he has received notice to that effect.

The landlord will have a statutory obligation to repair
under section 32 of the *Housing Act 1961* and must not
prevent reasonable access or discontinue the provision of

necessary services previously provided: the tenant must use the premises in a tenant-like manner, allow the landlord access to carry out repairs, use the premises as a private dwelling-house only and not assign or sub-let the whole or any part.

The Act provides ten cases under which the County Court may and two cases under which the court must, make an order for possession on the application of the landlord. The most important case is the discretionary one which enables the landlord to serve notice on the occupier where he has shown to the satisfaction of the housing authority that the dwelling-house is required to house an employee or prospective employee in agriculture, that he is unable to provide suitable alternative accommodation, that such provision is in the interests of efficient agriculture and the housing authority has offered suitable alternative accommodation.

The housing authority must use its best endeavours to provide suitable alternative accommodation where a landlord applies in writing and is able to show that he is unable to provide suitable alternative accommodation and that it is in the interests of efficient agriculture that such accommodation should be provided by the authority.

Advisory Committees may be approached by any of the parties for their advice which must be taken into account by the authority when determining whether it has an obligation to rehouse the occupier.

The housing authority must make its decision having regard to the advice given by the Committee, the urgency of the case, other needs for the accommodation available and the resources available to it.

Any breach of the statutory duty, such as it is, may be pursued by an action for damages against the housing authority.

Finally, three mandatory cases are provided under the *Rent Act 1977* (Cases 16, 17 and 18) where possession may be obtained for purposes connected with agriculture (see Section 8.4.3).

8.13   MULTIPLE OCCUPATION

Where a house is occupied by more than one family it is in multiple occupation and subject to special provisions re-

lating to repair and maintenance, overcrowding, provision
of standard amenities and means of escape from fire. A local
authority has power to make a *management order* appointing
a manager to be responsible for compliance with the regulations, a copy of which must be displayed in the house: this
may be followed by a *control order* under which the local
authority takes control.

Special grants are available towards the provision of standard amenities.

8.14   REPAIRS, IMPROVEMENTS AND GRANTS

Legislators have attempted to ensure the proper maintenance
and improvement of the housing stock by a combination of
sanctions and incentives. Thus, local authorities have wide
powers to deal with dis-repair while various enactments have
offered some advantage to the landlord whose property is in
proper repair. More recently grants have been made available
for improvements which in turn have been rewarded by the
fixing of higher rent limits.

8.14.1   Repairs

The common law position relating to implied repairing terms
is not altogether certain. However, in the absence of express
terms to the contrary, there is an implied term in relation to
furnished (but not unfurnished) premises that they will be in
habitable condition when let. Similarly, where there is no
express duty on the tenants or any one of them, it is implied
that the landlord is responsible for the repair of the common
parts of a building let to a number of tenants.

It has been argued that the landlord's duty to repair does
not arise until the want or repair has been notified to him
although it is suggested that where the landlord expressly
or impliedly reserves a right of entry to inspect the condition of the premises, he will be responsible for the work
together with any consequences of his failure to do the
work, in any instance where he was, or should have been,
aware of the dis-repair.

In the case of most dwelling-houses, the position is now
controlled by statute. Sections 32 and 33 of the *Housing*

Act 1961 (with the limitations applied by Section 80 of the *Housing Act 1980*) govern the repairing obligations of landlords of dwelling-houses let on short leases. There are very limited exclusions or provisions for contracting out (one being the exclusion of the provisions from leases granted after the commencement of the *Housing Act 1980* to certain specified bodies). The sections are set out in full —

'32. Repairing obligations in short leases of dwelling-houses — (1) In any lease of a dwelling-house, being a lease to which this section applies, there shall be implied a covenant by the lessor —

(a) to keep in repair the structure and exterior of the dwelling-house (including drains, gutters and external pipes); and

(b) to keep in repair and proper working order the installations in the dwelling-house —

  (i) for the supply of water, gas and electricity, and for sanitation (including basins, sinks, baths and sanitary conveniences but not, except as aforesaid, fixtures, fittings and appliances for making use of the supply of water, gas or electricity), and

  (ii) for space heating or heating water,

and any covenant by the lessee for the repair of the premises (including any covenant to put in repair or deliver up in repair, to paint, point or render or to pay money in lieu of repairs by the lessee or on account of repairs by the lessor) shall be of no effect so far as it relates to the matters mentioned in paragraphs (a) and (b) of this subsection.

(2) The covenant implied by this section (hereinafter referred to as the lessor's repairing covenant) shall not be construed as requiring the lessor —

(a) to carry out any works or repairs for which the lessee is liable by virtue of his duty to use the premises in a tenant-like manner, or would be so liable apart from any express covenant on his part;

        (b) to rebuild or reinstate the premises in the case of destruction or damage by fire, or by tempest, flood, or other inevitable accident; or

        (c) to keep in repair or maintain anything which the lessee is entitled to remove from the dwelling-house;

and subsection (1) of this section shall not avoid any covenant by the lessee so far as it imposes on the lessee any of the requirements mentioned in paragraph (a) or paragraph (c) of this subsection.

(3) In determining the standard of repair required by the lessor's repairing covenant, regard shall be had to the age, character and prospective life of the dwelling-house and the locality in which it is situated.

(4) In any lease in which the lessor's repairing covenant is implied, there shall also be implied a covenant by the lessee that the lessor, or any person authorised by him in writing, may at reasonable times of the day, on giving twenty-four hours notice in writing to the occupier, enter the premises comprised in the lease for the purpose of viewing their condition and state of repair.

(5) In this and the next following section the following expressions have the meanings hereby respectively assigned to them, that is to say: —

"lease" includes an underlease, an agreement for a lease or underlease, and any other tenancy, but does not include a mortgage and "covenant", "demise" and "term" shall be construed accordingly;

"lease of a dwelling-house" means a lease whereby a building or part of a building is let wholly or mainly as a private dwelling, and the "dwelling-house" means that building or part of a building;

"lessee" and "lessor" means respectively the

person for the time being entitled to
the term of a lease and to the reversion
expectant thereon.

33.   Application of section 32 and restriction on contracting out — (1) Section thirty-two of this Act
applies, subject to the provisions of this section, to
any lease of a dwelling-house granted after the
passing of this Act, being a lease for a term of less
than seven years.

(2) For the purposes of this section a lease shall be
treated as a lease for a term of less than seven
years if it is determinable at the option of the
lessor before the expiration of seven years from
the commencement of the term, and, except
where the foregoing provisions of this subsection apply, shall not be so treated if it confers
on the lessee an option for renewal for a term
which, together with the original term, amounts
to seven years or more.

(3) Where a lease of a dwelling-house (hereinafter
referred to as "the new lease") is granted —

(a) to a person who when, or immediately
before the new lease is granted, is the lessee
under another lease of the dwelling-house, or

(b) to a person who was the lessee under another
lease of the dwelling-house which terminated
at some time before the new lease is granted
and who, between the termination of that
other lease and the grant of the new lease was
continuously in possession of the dwelling-
house or the rents or profits thereof,

the said section thirty-two shall not apply to the
new lease if —

(i) the new lease is a tenancy to which Part II of
the Landlord and Tenant Act, 1954, applies
and the other lease either is such a tenancy
or would be such a tenancy but for section
twenty-eight of the said Act; or

(ii) the other lease is not a lease to which the said section thirty-two applies and, in the case of a lease granted before the passing of this Act would not have been such a lease if granted after that date.

(4) The said section thirty-two does not apply to any lease of a dwelling-house which is a tenancy of an agricultural holding within the meaning of the Agricultural Holdings Act, 1948.

(5) In the application of this section to a lease granted for a term part of which falls before the grant, that part shall be left out of account and the lease shall be treated as a lease for a term commencing with the grant.

(6) The county court may, by order made with the consent of the parties concerned, authorise the inclusion in a lease, or in any agreement collateral to a lease, of provisions excluding or modifying in relation to the lease the provisions of the said section thirty-two with respect to the repairing obligations of the parties if it appears to the court, having regard to the other terms and conditions of the lease and to all the circumstances of the case, that it is reasonable to do so; and any provision so authorised shall have effect accordingly.

(7) Subject to the last foregoing subsection, any covenant or agreement, whether contained in a lease to which the said section thirty-two applies or in any agreement collateral to such a lease, shall be void so far as it purports to exclude or limit the obligations of the lessor or the immunities of the lessee under that section, or to authorise any forfeiture or impose on the lessee any penalty, disability or obligation, in the event of his enforcing or relying upon those obligations or immunities.

(8) The county court shall have jurisdiction to make a declaration that section thirty-two of this Act applies, or does not apply to a lease, whatever the net annual value of the property in question, and notwithstanding that the applicant for the declaration does not seek any relief other than the declaration.'

The question arises as to what remedies one party may have where the other party defaults. The landlord's right to forfeiture is subject to the ability of the court to grant relief to the tenant which is also available where the court is satisfied that a notice requiring internal decorative repairs to be carried out under section 147 of the *Law of Property Act 1925* is unreasonable. The landlord may claim damages for breach of covenant but only in so far as the value of the reversion is diminished. The tenant may seek an order for specific performance of the repairing covenant or claim damages from the landlord for failure to carry out repairs. More simply, where a tenant has been unable to persuade his landlord to carry out repair work after reasonable notice, he may arrange for the work to be done and deduct the cost thereof from rent due then or in the future.

Statutory nuisances

Section 92 of the *Public Health Act 1936* gives powers to local authorities to deal with 'statutory nuisances' defined as any premises in such a state as to be or any accumulation or deposit which is prejudicial to health or a nuisance. Noise and vibration have been added to the categories of statutory nuisance by the *Noise Abatement Act 1960*. 'Prejudicial to health' is defined as 'injurious or likely to cause injury to health'.

An abatement notice is served on the appropriate person by the local authority (in the case of a structural defect the notice must be served on the owner). The notice will usually specify the work considered necessary to abate the nuisance and must allow a reasonable time for the work to be carried out. Where no work is carried out, the authority may apply to the magistrates for a nuisance order. In addition to making the order, they may also impose costs and a fine. An option available to the local authority is to carry out the work and recover the cost from the person responsible therefor.

The *Public Health Act 1961* provides a speeded up version where it appears to the local authority that undue delay would occur if the 1936 procedure was followed. The local authority serves a notice on the landlord of its intention of carrying out the work within nine days unless the owner replies within seven days to the effect that he intends to do the work himself.

8.14.2   Unfit houses

Where a house is unfit in accordance with the statutory definition contained in the *Housing Act 1957*, the local authority must take one of two courses. Where the house is considered to be capable of repair at reasonable cost, it must serve a list of defects with an order to carry out work necessary to remedy the defects. Where the house is believed to be incapable of repair at reasonable cost, the authority may after allowing time for representations—serve a demolition order or a closing order. Where the houses in the area generally fall into this category the authority may decide to initiate a clearance area.

8.14.3   Fit houses

Where a house, though fit for human habitation, requires substantial repair to bring it up to a reasonable standard, a local authority may serve upon the person having control of the house a notice requiring him within a reasonable period not being less than twenty-one days, to execute works specified in the notice. Internal decorative repair is excluded from the items of disrepair which may be included. The procedure is similar to that for unfit houses but the notice is not limited by any specific reference to reasonable expense. In so far as the cost might be a factor in considering the requirement of the local authority, it appears that the comparison should be made in the light of the value of the house with vacant possession on completion of the work and not on the value subject to the existing tenancy.

8.14.4 **Improvement**

Except where there is an absolute prohibition against the protected or statutory tenant carrying out improvements, it is implied by the *Housing Act 1980* that consent to such work shall not be unreasonably withheld, although the landlord may impose reasonable conditions. The purpose of the restatement of this provision previously contained in the *Landlord and Tenant Act 1927* is to facilitate the work of improvement by tenants who may now be eligible for grants in certain cases. The definition of improvements includes

1. Additions and alterations to the landlord's fixtures and fittings
2. Additions and alterations connected with the provision of services
3. Erection of any wireless or television aerial
4. External decorations (but not where the landlord is responsible for exterior repair or decoration)

Improvements may be carried out by the landlord: where the tenant refuses his consent, the landlord may apply to the County Court for an order to enter and carry out the works. In considering the application, the court is required to have regard to all the circumstances and in particular to —

(a) Any disadvantage to the tenant that might be expected to result from the works, and
(b) The accommodation that might be available for him while the works are carried out, and
(c) The age and health of the tenant

but the court shall not take into account the means or resources of the tenant.

In Housing Action and General Improvement Areas, the local authority may serve a provisional notice on the owner of the dwelling-house, on the tenant and on any other person having a legal interest where it is satisfied that the provision of any missing standard amenities can be achieved at reasonable cost. This is a prerequisite to the compulsory procedure for improvement and the notice must specify a time and place at which objections may be made following which the local authority may proceed with the service of a final notice requiring the specified work to be carried out, normally within twelve months. The owner may decide to comply with the order in which case he is entitled to the appropriate grant and a loan for the balance of the costs subject to the owner showing that he is in a position to meet the capital repayments and interest charges. The owner may decide that he does not wish to carry out the work in which case he has six months in which to serve a purchase notice on the local authority. Where the period elapses without service of a purchase notice the local authority may serve a further notice asking whether the owner intends to do the work and where the result is unsatisfactory may serve a notice stating that it proposes to do the work and may proceed after 21 days or may delay action until twelve months have elapsed. The local authority is entitled to recover the costs of the work from the owner who is not allowed to benefit from any grant.

Where the dwelling-house is not in a designated area, the tenant may make a formal request to the local authority for the provision of missing standard amenities and the authority may then commence the procedure outlined above.

8.14.5 Grants

In an effort to conserve the housing stock, grants have been made available by successive governments and administered through local authorities.

The basic criteria of eligibility and the range of grants available are set out by the *Housing Act 1974* as amended by the Act of 1980.

Grants are normally available to owner occupiers where the rateable value is less than £225 although this limit does not apply if the house is in a Housing Action Area or the works are for the benefit of a disabled occupier.

In addition, owners of tenanted houses are eligible as are tenants of houses where the landlord certifies that the house will be available for letting throughout the five year period immediately following completion of the grant-aided work. In the case of houses in Housing Action Areas the certificate must be for not less than a seven year period.

To qualify for an improvement grant, the Act requires that the house should, on completion of the proposed work, be in reasonable repair having regard to its age, character and locality. In addition to having the 'standard amenities' (consisting of a fixed bath or shower, washbasin, sink, inside W.C. and hot and cold water to the appliances as appropriate) the house should

   (i) Be substantially free from damp
  (ii) Have adequate natural lighting and ventilation in each habitable room
 (iii) Have adequate and safe provision throughout for artificial lighting and have sufficient electric socket outlets
 (iv) Be provided with adequate drainage
  (v) Have satisfactory internal arrangement
 (vi) Be in a stable structural condition
(vii) Have satisfactory facilities for preparing and cooking food
(viii) Have adequate facilities for heating
 (ix) Have proper facilities for the storage of solid fuel where necessary and for the storage of refuse and
  (x) Satisfy the Building Regulations for thermal insulation of the roof spaces

There are four classes of grant, as follows (see Table 8.2).

Improvement grants are awarded at the discretion of the Council. The amount available is 75% of the maximum approved cost of the work where the house is in a Housing Action Area, 65% in a General Improvement Area and 50% elsewhere. In order to qualify, the house should have an estimated further life of at least 30 years on completion of the work.

Intermediate grants are available as of right to ensure that a house has standard amenities and is in a satisfactory state of repair. The grants are available for houses in General Improvement and Housing Action Areas and the same percentages apply.

Repairs grants are available also in General Improvement and Housing Action Areas where the house has the standard amenities: again, the same percentages apply.

Finally, Special Grants are available for houses in multi-

Table 8.2 Summary of grant-aid

Type of grant		Maximum approved cost (£)	Housing Action Areas	General Improvement Areas	Other areas
Improvement	A*	8500	75%	65%	50%
	B†	5500			
Intermediate					
Bath		285			
Washbasin		110			
Sink		285	65%	75%	75%
HC to bath		360			
washbasin		190			
sink		240			
WC		430			
Repairs		2500			
Repairs		4000	75%	65%	

* Higher maxima apply where the grant is intended to enable houses having three or more storeys to be converted to flats.
† The normal maximum is £5500 but this may be increased as shown, principally where the house is in a Housing Action Area or where the work is to be carried out by virtue of a notice served under section 9 or 16 of the *Housing Act 1957*.

occupation to enable the owner to provide basic amenities and fire escapes.

Under these provisions, substantial amounts may be obtained as grants from the local authority. In certain exceptional cases, the grant may be increased to 90%.

It is often possible to obtain the balance of the cost in the form of a loan from the local authority or from a building society.

8.15 LICENCES

A licence gives a right to occupy but conveys no legal estate or interest and may not give exclusive possession. This last point is less important than it once was. It is clear that without exclusive occupation a tenancy cannot exist but it does not follow that exclusive possession will necessarily be conclusive in defeating a claim to the existence of a licence.

The importance of the distinction in the occupation of residential accommodation is that the Rent Acts do not in general apply to licences (although see the provisions relating to restricted contracts, page 137). While it is not possible to contract out of the provisions of the Acts, it may be possible to arrange the transaction in such a way that it falls outside the legislation. The transaction must be a genuine one and not a sham merely to avoid the Acts. Denning M. R. described the test in this way

'All the circumstances have to be worked out. Eventually the answer depends on the nature and quality of the occupancy. Was it intended that the occupier should have a stake in the room or did he have only permission for himself personally to occupy the room, whether under a contract or not, in which case he is a licensee.' (Marchant *v.* Charters 1977)

The *Protection from Eviction Act 1977* specifically gives protection to, *inter alia*

'a licensee, whether or not he is a lessee under a restricted contract and whether or not he has exclusive possession of any part of the premises'.

8.16 LONG TENANCIES AT LOW RENTS

The Rent Acts do not extend to long tenancies at low rents. For this purpose a long tenancy is defined as one for more than 21 years and which cannot be terminated before that time.

A low rent is one less than two-thirds of the rateable value, payments for maintenance, repairs, rates, insurance and services to be excluded.

Such tenancies enabled the landlord to obtain possession and to claim for items of disrepair until Part I of the *Landlord and Tenant Act 1954* gave the occupying tenant some protection.

Detailed provisions require that any notice served by the landlord should contain proposals for the terms to be incorporated in a statutory tenancy or give information as to the grounds on which he proposes to rely in an application to the court for an order for possession.

Where the tenant has not complied with the repairing covenants of his lease and agreement is not reached between the parties, the court will intervene to determine the repairs to be carried out by the tenant. Should the landlord take proceedings more than seven months before the end of the term, the tenant may comply with any order made or elect to treat the term as coming to an end. In the latter case his liability will be limited to the payment of costs.

The *Leasehold Reform Act 1967* attempted a much more radical solution by enabling an occupying tenant of a house (but not a flat) within certain rateable value limits to serve a notice to acquire the freehold interest or to extend the lease for a further 50 years subject to payment of a 'modern' ground rent.

The valuation rules ensure that the enfranchising tenant pays only for the site and this subject to certain assumptions many of which have been the subject of interpretation by the Lands Tribunal.

The original Act remains the principal Act though certain amendments have been made by the 1979 Act of the same name, by the *Rent Act 1977* and by various Housing Acts.

FURTHER READING

Aldridge, T. M. (1980) *The Housing Act 1980*, Oyez Publishing, London.
Macey, J. P. and Baker, C. V. (1978) Housing Management. 2nd edn, Estates Gazette, London.
Partington, M. (1980) *Landlord and Tenant*, Weidenfeld and Nicholson, London.
Pettit, P. H. (1981) *Private Sector Tenancies*, Butterworths, London.
West, W. A. (1979) *The Law of Housing*, Estates Gazette, London.

CHAPTER 9

Outgoings and service charges

9.1 INTRODUCTION

In this chapter the range of expenditures incurred by the landlord and tenant are considered together with the part played by the property manager in ensuring that the premises are maintained in satisfactory condition.

He may initiate and supervise work which is the responsibility of the landlord and ensure that the tenant performs the repairing obligations placed on him by the lease.

He will determine the amount and the extent of insurance cover and ensure that the policy remains in force.

He will be responsible for the apportionment of service charges and for collection of the amount due.

Finally, he will have responsibilities where the landlord is required by statute to undertake or to contribute to the cost of certain repairs, modifications or improvements.

9.2 REPAIRS AND MAINTENANCE

Repairs and maintenance are concerned with the standards necessary to maintain the premises in an acceptable condition in accordance with the provisions contained in the lease and in a state to command the rent. Repairs are undertaken to remedy defects while maintenance preserves the premises and keeps fixtures and fixed equipment in working order.

9.2.1 Liability

The responsibility for repair and maintenance is usually provided for in the lease between the parties. Where the

lease is silent, responsibility is determined by implication
or reference to common law.

It is essential for the property manager to have the lease
itself or a copy to enable him to interpret the responsibility
for work required.

It is insufficient and may be dangerous to rely on extracts
from the lease or notes of the covenant.

In lettings of residential properties the landlord's responsibility for repair and maintenance may be laid down by
statute: in some circumstances the landlord may be required
to carry out improvements also.

9.2.2   Condition on entry

A schedule of state of repair and condition should be prepared prior to the commencement of a tenancy by the landlord's agent and agreed with the tenant or his agent unless
the tenant has accepted full repairing liabilities. It serves as an
historical record and assists in the resolution of differences of
opinion. It may also provide a firm basis for a claim for dilapidations on the expiration of a tenancy.

9.2.3   Inspection and notice to repair

It is usual for a lease to contain a covenant by the tenant
to permit the landlord personally or by an agent and with
or without workmen or others to enter at any time during
the term at reasonable times after giving notice in writing
to view the state and condition of the premises. Provision
is also made for service of notice on the lessee to remedy
any defects found as a result of such inspection and for the
work to be carried out by the landlord at the tenant's expense
where the tenant fails to do so.

For this purpose, a right of entry is reserved and provision
made for recovery from the tenant of the costs of carrying
out the work together with any charges incurred.

The agent should make use of the power to inspect to
carry out regular inspection as part of his routine management. Adequate records should be maintained to enable

the agent to quote the date of inspection, the condition in which the building was found and the action taken together with the outcome.

Such information improves the quality of management, instils confidence in the landlord and is often crucial where action has to be taken against the tenant.

The landlord may choose to exercise a right of re-entry reserved in the lease by serving an appropriate notice on the tenant. Section 146 of the *Law of Property Act 1925* regulates the procedure and enables the tenant to apply to the court for relief from forfeiture (see Chapter 5).

9.3   INSURANCE

The owner of a property will wish to be in a position to reinstate the building in the event of damage or destruction. This is usually achieved by entering into a contract of indemnity with an insurance company whereby, in exchange for an annual premium, the company undertakes to pay for work necessary to repair or replace the building up to the full amount covered. The extent and amount of the cover will be determined by the owner, the tenant, or may be specified by a provision in the lease.

9.3.1   Extent of cover

The buildings may be insured against damage by fire only or for other risks also, such as storm and tempest, flood, impact and subsidence. It is possible and usual to include in the cover a sum for professional fees for rebuilding services and loss of rent for a stipulated period. A business tenant would probably wish to insure for additional items such as consequential loss, the effect of business interruption and loss of or damage to fixtures, fittings and stock.

9.3.2   Sum insured

Insurance cover should normally be for the full estimated cost of replacement. In addition to the cost of rebuilding, other charges incurred would include supporting and keeping watertight adjoining buildings exposed by the damage, demolition of unsafe portions, compliance with additional requirements of the planning authority or of building regulations and loss of rent for the period of rebuilding. In times of rising costs, it is prudent to reconsider the adequacy of cover every year: many insurance companies now provide for automatic increases by means of 'indexing' whereby the cover is adjusted annually by reference to an index of building costs. Where a property is insufficiently covered the insured is regarded as his own insurer for the shortfall: not only are total losses affected but a claim for partial loss would be scaled down also.

The property manager should consult the lease for provisions relating to the insurance of tenant's improvements and should ensure that adequate cover is maintained where the landlord is responsible for effecting insurance or where he is able to stipulate the sum for which the tenant should insure. Unless the building is totally destroyed, value added tax is likely to be payable on the rebuilding or repair work and it would be prudent for the property manager to consult the owner as to whether an additional sum should be included for this contingency.

Older buildings may cost considerably more to repair or rebuild than their modern counterparts and insurance on a replacement basis may be prohibitive. Examples are multi-storey mills and many churches: in such cases it is possible to negotiate cover assuming replacement with a modern equivalent subject to safeguards for both parties generally and in particular where there is a partial loss only. Even so, the insurance premium will be relatively large and possibly in excess of the rental value. Third party liability is necessary to protect the landlord against public liability or claims made as a result of his duties, if any, under specific enactments, e.g. the *Occupier's Liability Act 1957* and the *Defective Premises Act 1972*.

9.4   SERVICE CHARGES

9.4.1   **Purpose**

Service charges are charges for those items the execution of which is, under the terms of the lease, the responsibility of the owner but the total cost of which is to be met by the occupier. In buildings or developments occupied by a number of tenants, the items would include not only the shared services such as toilets, heating etc., shared areas such as lifts, staircases and malls, but also the insurance and maintenance of the building as a whole.

The outgoings may be payable in this way because it is more convenient or practicable or more efficient. It would be impracticable for each of several occupiers of an office block to decorate his own external wall or for the tenant immediately below the roof to collect a proportion of any cost of repair from all the other tenants in the building. Similarly, the landlord may have a maintenance force in his employ when it is likely to be quicker and more efficient for him to undertake the work initially.

9.4.2   Apportionment of costs

Where the lease provides for work to be carried out or expenses to be incurred by the landlord on behalf of the tenant, such costs are recoverable by the imposition of a service charge. In the case of a shop unit within a shopping centre, the recoverable expenses would probably be stipulated by reference to the types of expenditure envisaged. Among these would be included supervision and management of the centre, the cost of employing management staff, their office and storage accommodation, telephones, rates and the costs of heating, lighting, repairing, decorating and cleaning.

The lease will lay down the basis on which the costs are to be apportioned: the most common method is on the basis of floor area where the charge is that proportion of the total costs which the floor area of the unit bears to the overall floor area. An equitable basis would provide for a differential rate in respect of common parts and ancillary accommodation such as storage, basement areas or garaging. In some cases, each tenant pays an equal proportion of the costs of services attributable to the common areas.

Apportionment by reference to rent paid is likely to be less satisfactory, especially where the same building carries permission for a variety of uses and therefore has a range of rental values. Similarly, the use of rateable values is unsatisfactory as well as being objectionable on the ground that the basis of calculation is outside the control of the interested parties.

The service charge may include sums to be placed in a contingency fund to provide for periodic replacement or renewal of more expensive items.

Unless part of the service charge is payable in advance, the landlord may be forced to provide substantial sums to meet running costs pending receipt of service charges from tenants. Many leases stipulate that an estimated amount should be paid in advance, the remainder to be paid when expenditure is proved by the production of audited accounts. Such a practice is unsatisfactory where a particular sum is specified as it will soon be inadequate.

9.4.3   Statutory intervention

An increase in the number of flats, both purpose-built and converted, held on long leases has resulted in the imposition of service charges on a larger scale than hitherto.

Undoubtedly, some landlords took advantage of strict and tightly drawn covenants in their favour to present bills for charges which could neither be substantiated nor challenged. Legislation to combat the abuses and to regularize procedures was first passed in 1972 and has been replaced by Schedule 19 of the *Housing Act 1980*, the whole of which is now operative.

The Act defined a service charge as a sum payable as part of or in addition to rent directly or indirectly for services, repairs and maintenance insurance and the landlord's costs of management. The relevant costs are the actual or estimated costs incurred or to be incurred to be taken into account only in so far as the costs and the standard of services are reasonable. Where service charges are paid before the relevant costs are incurred, there is provision for adjustment when the costs are known.

Where works are to be carried out at a cost in excess of £25 for each flat in the building or £500, in total, whichever is the greater, the landlord must obtain two estimates, one from someone unconnected with the landlord, and consult each tenant. Consultation may be directly with each tenant or by display of information in the building, in each case with copies of the estimates. Where there is a recognized tenants' association, similar information must be supplied to the secretary. Work must not be started within one month of notice to the tenants unless it is urgent. Where a court is satisfied that a landlord acted reasonably, it may dispense with some or all of the requirements for consultation.

A tenant is empowered to request a written summary of costs from the landlord with provisions as to time and certification. Any breach of the provisions may incur a fine not exceeding £500, in addition to which the excess expenditure may not be recoverable.

The report of an action for forfeiture of the lease of a flat on the grounds of non-payment of rent and service charge makes interesting reading in Woodtrek Ltd *v.* Jezek 1982. The case proceeded by reference to the 1972 and 1974 Acts, the provisions of both of which have now been replaced by the *Housing Act 1980*. These changes affect only the details of the judgment, not its determination. The major part of the judgment concerns the landlords claim for payment of an interim service charge and the attempt to obtain forfeiture on non-payment. A review of the then current legislation left the judge in no doubt as to the futility of the claim in the absence of receipts or other substantiation of the amount due. As far as arrears of rent were concerned, the judge held that, although the proceedings were technically justified the behaviour of the landlords left a great deal to be desired and he granted relief from forfeiture.

The provisions do not apply to local authorities, development corporations, county councils or certain public bodies unless the tenancy is a long tenancy, when modified provisions apply. Whilst provisions in a lease cannot override the statutory provisions, it may be that the lease itself creates additional restrictions on the landlord: for example where the lease itself provides only for expenditure already incurred to be recovered or restricts the periodic amount to be recovered in advance.

9.5   FEES

9.5.1   Responsibility for payment

In calculating the service charge payable by each tenant, charges will be incurred in the form of surveyors' accountants' and auditors' fees and possibly of solicitors' fees also. These charges are normally apportioned among the tenants as part of the service charge.

FURTHER READING

Building Cost Information Service (1981) Guide to house rebuilding costs for insurance valuation, Royal Institution of Chartered Surveyors, London.

Davis, Belfield and Everest (eds) (1983) *Spon's Architects' and Builders' Price Book*, E. and F. N. Spon, London.

Dent, C. (1974) *Construction Cost Appraisal*, George Godwin, London.

West, W. A. (1979) The law of dilapidations. *Estates Gazette.*

CHAPTER 10

Planned maintenance

10.1   INTRODUCTION

Too often the property manager is not one of the members of the design team when a new building is planned: his wide knowledge of the problems of buildings in use would justify his inclusion.

The contribution which he was able to make would often improve the usefulness of the completed building and increase the flexibility of use, thus enhancing the prospects of finding and keeping a tenant or tenants. He should be able to make significant suggestions regarding materials and layout. Such matters affect capital and rental values and the cost of maintenance procedures. While his exclusion is understandable it is also true that his experience in the management of buildings and estates would be invaluable in identifying problems inherent in the design which would affect the use and which may depress capital and rental values and also net incomes.

The intention of the developer may play a part in design considerations. Where he is building for sale he will be anxious to present an attractive product but will be less concerned with deterioration and maintenance. His view may well be different where he intends to hold the building as a long term investment then, not only will he not wish to incur any unnecessary expense, he will seek to avoid troublesome maintenance, especially where this may have an effect on rental value. Where he intends to occupy the premises he will tend to weigh the alternatives of immediate capital costs against deferred maintenance expenses and make a financial judgment.

In the case of developments of factories, warehouses and offices where funds are provided by institutional investors, there is already a measure of control directed towards producing a building which will let readily. The present element of over-supply and therefore choice enables the prospective tenant to be more selective than in the past especially where he is professionally advised. There is more incentive now than at any time in the past 30 or so years to offer for letting a building which is attractive, sound, energy saving and as free of maintenance as is consistent with reasonable initial costs.

Shop premises will be less affected by such considerations where location is the critical factor. Poor construction has been less of a problem with such buildings, no doubt because the major cost of developing a prime site is the value attributed to the land, the rental value is therefore less sensitive to an increase in the cost of construction.

The quality of design, the materials used and the standard of workmanship all combine to affect maintenance costs during the life of a building. The ideal building would be one designed and built to a high specification and consequently requiring the minimum attention during its life. It is unlikely that such a building would be the most economically viable: the typical building is much more likely to be a compromise between a reasonable standard of design and construction and a modest level of maintenance expenditure. Each decision made at the design stage has implications for maintenance costs and it is in the interests of owner and occupier that the correct balance is achieved.

10.2 THE FUNCTION OF THE PROPERTY MANAGER

In the context of maintenance, the function of the property manager is to maintain the building to an appropriate and acceptable standard at reasonable cost and with the minimum of inconvenience to the occupier.

The standard of maintenance may be laid down in the lease and be the responsibility of the lessor or lessee or may be determined by the requirements of the client related to his ability to pay for the work and by the type of building. A building visited by the occupier's customers may be maintained beyond the standard strictly necessary in order to create a favourable impression with those customers whilst a manufacturing unit is likely to be maintained only to the level necessary to provide continuity of production and satisfactory conditions for workers: execution of all but urgent repairs and maintenance is likely to be deferred to the period of the annual shut-down.

During the life of a building, the amount spent on maintenance is likely to be significant when compared with the initial or capital cost. It is therefore desirable to prepare a provisional periodic work-list flexible enough to ensure that the work is done only if the necessity is confirmed by inspection. A swift response to unscheduled failures will remain necessary though regular inspections are likely to reduce such occurrences. The technical manual referred to in Chapter 2 will be invaluable in giving precise instructions to the maintenance team.

In most cases the property manager will be exercising his authority on behalf of the landlord and, on occasion, may find it necessary to carry out work which is the responsibility of the tenant where the tenant fails to do so and where the building is falling into disrepair as a result. In such cases, it will be helpful in any action for the recovery of expenses incurred to have detailed survey notes and photographs in addition to copies of letters and records of telephone conversations.

The approach to maintenance will now be considered in more detail.

10.3   DEFINITION OF MAINTENANCE

There are numerous definitions of 'maintenance' but it is proposed to use the one offered by the Committee on Building Maintenance of the Department of the Environment contained in its report published in 1972 which was based on a definition contained in BS 3811: 1964

'Building maintenance is work undertaken in order to keep, restore or improve every facility i.e. every part of a building, its services and surrounds, to a currently accepted standard and to sustain the utility and value of the facility'

The committee added the word 'improve' to reflect the fact that most buildings have long life expectancies and acceptable standards of amenity and performance will rise substantially over their lifetime as a result of one or more of the following —

(a) Statutory requirements, e.g. safety, health and welfare provisions
(b) Regulations of statutory undertakers
(c) The need to maintain a public image
(d) Steps taken to maintain rental values

10.4   THE MAINTENANCE PLAN

The plan should be comprehensive and systematic, encompassing both short and medium term considerations. The programme should be based on a sound knowledge of the building and have regard to the following.

10.4.1   The life of the building

The length of the further period for which a building will last should be estimated even though the estimate may be revised at some time in the future. Regard may be paid to the physical life or to the functional or economic life (usually a shorter period). Experience suggests that towards the end of its physical life a building may present major problems requiring 'first-aid' maintenance and that even then it will attract only marginal occupiers. Perhaps, then, it would be preferable to consider the economic life of the building (coinciding largely with its functional life) which may be defined as the period during which a satisfactory tenant would be prepared to occupy the premises which would not require appreciably more maintenance than newer but otherwise similar buildings. Where the location is satisfactory, it is often feasible to extend the economic life by undertaking a major refurbishment of the building. For example, very attractive offices have been created out of well-sited period dwellings and from 19th century warehouses. Where a building is listed, or where there are planning or legal problems, it may be essential to consider upgrading the existing building even though it would be more viable to redevelop the site.

The plant and machinery in the building (e.g. central

heating installation, lifts) are likely to have a much shorter life than the building itself.

10.4.2 The standard to be achieved

Where the building is one which will be in great demand because of its location, design or facilities there should be no difficulty in setting and meeting an appropriately high standard of maintenance. But not all buildings fall into that category and it may be necessary to set a much lower standard, where only essential work is carried out. Where refurbishment is not practicable, a building may be assigned one life span with a good standard of maintenance followed by a further period where it is recognized that the same quality of tenant cannot be attracted and that a consequent lowering of the standard of maintenance will not deter the poorer type of tenant.

10.4.3 The financial implications

Periodic maintenance items should be costed on an annual basis and related to the income available. Where the cash requirement for refurbishment or other major work is too great to be met from income there should be a reasonable possibility of adequate funds becoming available before the proposal is included in the plan. Such work can often be funded on the basis of a loan granted on the considerably greater capital value of the building when the work has been completed.

10.4.4 Responsibility for maintenance

The property manager may have direct control of maintenance work but more often he will have only a supervisory role in ensuring that the tenant performs his covenant to maintain the property. Regular inspections should be made for this purpose, if necessary by invoking the right of inspection reserved in the majority of leases.

10.5 FINANCIAL POLICY

The property manager should take the earliest opportunity to acquaint himself with the policy of his clients and with their expectations. He is then in a position to take the initiative in devising a long term plan with its financial implications for discussion with his clients. The objective in most cases is to maximize the return from the property which requires a positive approach. But the property manager should beware of placing himself or his clients in a financial straightjacket — costs change over a period as do rental values and it is notoriously difficult to forecast either. The aim should be for the plan to be indicative and evolutionary rather than rigid or restrictive.

10.6   BUDGETARY PROVISION

Approval of the financial plan will greatly facilitate the periodic allocation of sufficient sums for its implementation. The client is likely to prepare his budget on an annual basis and may expect to allocate a similar sum for maintenance each year. Such an approach would not recognize the probability of fluctuations in expenditure from one year to the next, e.g. renewal of a roof covering at twenty year intervals or external painting every five years will impose unequal demands on finance. Nevertheless, there is no reason why expenditure should not be equated as far as possible by appropriate timing and spacing of the more expensive maintenance items provided there is no conflict with the principles of good management.

10.7   INDIFFERENCE LEVELS

When carrying out repairs to an existing building the choice of solutions is limited: nevertheless, it is often necessary to make a decision between carrying out a repair and undertaking a renewal.

Example
Where a renewal would cost £1000 and an annual repair to the same item £200, it is likely that the renewal would be preferred: if, on the other hand, the annual cost of repair was likely to be as little as £25, then no doubt the periodic inconvenience would be accepted. Figure 10.1 looks more closely at the relationship by comparing capital and revenue

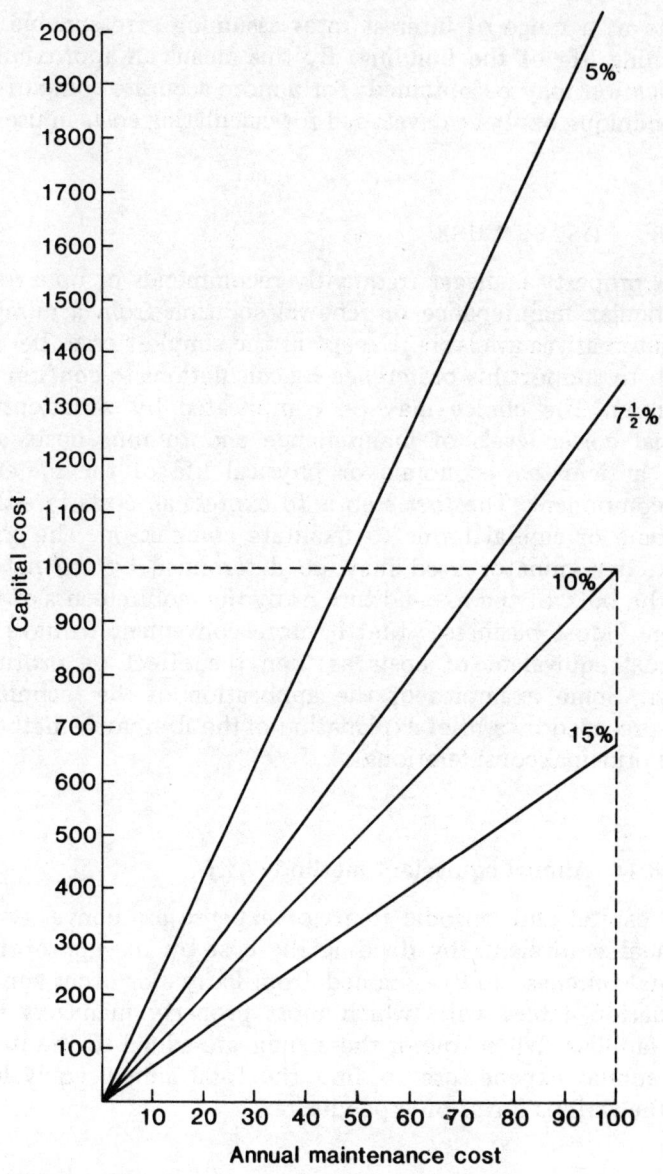

Fig. 10.1 Indifference levels. Where the opportunity cost of capital is known, the annual cost of maintenance may be compared with the capital replacement cost. For example, where the cost of capital is 10% and the annual maintenance cost £100, it will be cheaper to replace rather than repair at any cost under £1000

costs at a range of interest rates assuming a reasonable remaining life of the building. By this means an approximate indication may be obtained: for a more accurate comparison a technique has been developed for calculating costs in use.

10.8   COSTS IN USE

The property manager frequently recommends or opts for a particular maintenance or renewal solution from a number of alternatives available. Except in the simplest cases he will wish to support his preference by calculations to confirm his opinion. The choice may be complicated by variations in initial costs, levels of maintenance and running costs and the anticipated economic or physical life of the material or component. The first step is to express all costs in either income or capital terms to facilitate comparison. The common denominator used may be determined by the nature of the bulk of the expenditure or by the requirements of the client. Most businesses find it more convenient to have an annual equivalent of costs as then the effect on profit is clear. Some examples of the application of the technique are preceded by a brief explanation of the alternative methods and principal considerations.

10.8.1   Annual equivalent method (AE)

All capital and periodic items of expense are converted to annual equivalents by dividing the cost by the appropriate years' purchase (YP) obtained from Parry's or other similar valuation tables with which most property managers will be familiar. When found, these sums are added to the items of annual expenditure to find the total annual equivalent of the various forms of expenditure.

Example
The annual equivalent of a capital cost of £10000 for re-covering a flat roof which is then expected to last for 15 years, assuming that the discount rate is 8% (see Section

10.7.3) is

$$\frac{£10\,000}{\text{YP 15 years at 8\%}}$$

$$= \frac{£10\,000}{8.5595 \text{ (from tables)}}$$

$$= £1168 \text{ per annum}$$

The same result would be obtained by multiplying the capital sum by a figure representing interest and sinking fund provisions (see Section 10.8.4).

In the above example

Capital cost		£10 000
Annual interest at 8%	0.08	
Sinking fund to replace £1 in 15 years at 8% (from tables)	0.036 829 5	0.116 829 5
		£1168 per annum

10.8.2   Present value basis (PV)

Instead of reducing all expenditure to an annual basis, all costs are capitalized so as to arrive at the present capital value of all payments made or to be made in the future. Annual and periodic payments are converted into equivalent capital sums and added to any capital expenditure.

Example
It is anticipated that £750 per annum will be spent on servicing a lift installation which will cost £20 000 to install. The lift is expected to have an economic life of twelve years.

Initial expenditure		£20 000
Annual maintenance	£750	
Present value of series of 12 annual payments, discounted at 8% (i.e. YP 12 years at 8%)	7.5361	5652
Present value of total expenditure		£25 652

10.8.3   Selection of the rate of interest

Whether future expenditure is being discounted or capital costs converted to annual equivalents, an appropriate rate of interest will need to be selected. The rate of interest will vary with the credit-worthiness of the borrower, the necessity for him to borrow, his internal rate of return and the compensation required in the form of higher interest rates for the erosion of the purchasing power of capital inflation. To the extent that the process is intended to provide a comparison on which to base a decision, the rate of interest adopted is not critical. However, it should be borne in mind that where high rates are selected, recurring costs will tend to show up in a favourable light while low rates will favour initial costs. In the examples that follow, a rate of 8% has been adopted throughout.

10.8.4   Sinking fund and tax

Where a component has a limited life, consideration should be given to the provision of a sinking fund to replace the component at the end of that life. The sinking fund provision becomes significant where the life is less than, say, 40 years. In both the annual equivalent and the present value methods considered above, there is provision for investment in a sinking fund to accrue at the same rate as that adopted for discounting. However, because neither annual payments to a sinking fund nor interest received on the sinking fund instalments are exempt from tax, it is unlikely that the use of the same rate will be appropriate. A different rate of interest on sinking fund payments may be allowed for and provision made for the effects of tax on both the annual increments to the fund and the interest payments accruing to it. The following calculations illustrate the approach. In each case the discount rate has been taken at 8%, the gross interest on sinking fund 6% and the revenue tax liability 50%. The life of the component has been assumed to be 20 years.

(a) *Annual equivalent basis*

8% discount rate   0.08

Interest on sinking fund of 6%
   subject to tax at 50% net
   rate 3% sinking fund to
   produce £1 in 20 years
   at 3% (from tables)   0.0372157

Gross up where provided from
   income taxed at 50%

$$\left(\frac{100}{100-50}\right) \times 2 \qquad\qquad 0.0744314$$

Multiplier to find annual
   equivalent of capital sum   0.1544314

(b) *Present value basis*

Years' purchase is derived from the formula $1/(i + s)$ where i is the interest rate, s the sinking fund and si the net return on sinking fund.

To allow for the effect of tax on the sinking fund payments, that part of the formula must be increased by $100/(100-50)$ or z.

The formula becomes

$$\frac{1}{i + z(s)}$$

and in its expanded form

$$1 \Big/ \left\{ i + z \left[\frac{si}{(1 + si)^n - 1} \right] \right\}$$

Substituting the details in this example

$$\text{YP} = 1 \Big/ \left\{ 0.08 + 2 \left[\frac{0.03}{1.03^{20} - 1} \right] \right\}$$

$$= \frac{1}{0.08 + 2(0.0372157)}$$

$$= \frac{1}{0.08 + 0.0744314}$$

$$= \frac{1}{0.1544314}$$

$$6.475367$$

being the YP for 20 years to show a return of 8% on the remunerative rate and a net interest on the sinking fund payments of 3% allowing for tax at 50% on the annual payments.

It will be noted that the figure calculated in (a) is the reciprocal of the figure calculated in (b).

10.8.5 Life of the component

The life of the component is an essential element in each calculation. A freehold interest in land may be treated as a perpetual life not subject to depreciation unless planning or other artificial restrictions exist. On the other hand, most components are wasting assets. It is important to identify the economic life rather than the physical life of a component.

10.8.6 Costs

Costs to be incurred in the future may be estimated on the basis of current charges or an attempt made to predict the level of charges likely at some future date. The latter course is problematical and, for most purposes, unnecessary. The use of current costs will normally be sufficient for comparison purposes.

10.8.7 The technique in practice

The following examples are designed to illustrate the use of the technique.

Example
A leaseholder is considering the renewal of a central heating system at a cost of £3000, the anticipated running costs (fuel and maintenance) being £1200 per annum. He has been advised that the provision of double glazing at a cost of £1500 will reduce the running costs to £900 per annum. Compare the alternatives, on annual equivalent and capital value bases assuming an economic life for the installation of 25 years and a lease term exceeding this period. Do not provide a separate sinking fund and ignore the incidence of tax.

Solution

(a) Without double glazing

Initial cost	£3000	
AE over 25 years at 8%	0.0936788	281
Running costs, per annum		1200
AE of all costs		£1481

(b) With double glazing

Initial cost — heating and glazing	£4500	
AE over 25 years at 8%	0.0936788	422
Running costs, per annum		900
AE of all costs		£1322

The higher initial cost when providing double glazing is shown to be justified by the substantial saving in running costs.

The calculations on a capital basis are now shown.

(a) Without double glazing

Initial cost		£3000
Running costs, per annum	1200	
YP 25 years at 8%	10.6748	12810
PV of all costs		£15810

(b) With double glazing

Initial cost (heating and glazing)		4500
Running costs, per annum	900	
YP 25 years at 8%	10.6748	9607
PV of all costs		£14107

These calculations confirm that the higher initial cost results in an overall saving. The saving is likely to be higher than shown as it is reasonable to assume that fuel costs will continue to rise.

Example

A has purchased an unexpired term of 30 years in a leasehold interest for a premium of £47000, the annual rent being £1000. What are the capital and annual implications of the purchase: a sinking fund can be invested to show 8% subject to tax at 50%.

Solution
By calculation, the YP for 30 years at 8% and 4% subject to tax at 50% is 8.6460 and the sinking fund, adjusted for tax, is 0.0356602

(a) PV basis

Premium		£47000
Rent reserved	1000	
YP 30 years at 8% and 4% (tax 50%)	8.6460	8646
PV of all costs		£55646

(b) AE basis

Premium	47000	
Sinking fund over 30 years at 4% (tax 50%)	0.0356602	1676
Rent reserved		1000
AE of all costs		£2676

Example
A manufacturer wishes to expand his operations for which he requires additional space. He may purchase an adjoining site for £17000 and erect a building at a cost of £125000 including fees or he may take a lease of a convenient building of similar floor area on a 15 year lease at a rent of £9000 per annum with a premium of £20000. Compare the relative costs. If he elects to build, the factory will be ready for occupation in one year's time.
AE basis — build

Cost of land	£ 17000
Cost of building	125000
Total cost	142000
Defer one year at 8%	0.9259259
	£ 131481

Annual equivalent at 8%		0.08
AE of total cost		£ 10 518

AE basis — rent

Rent reserved, per annum		9 000
Premium	20 000	
Divide by YP 15 years at 8% and 4% (tax 50%)	5.559 2	3 598
AE of rent and premium		£ 12 598

As the lives of the alternatives vary, the PV basis would be inappropriate. The manufacturer will see from the calculations that not only would he pay a higher annual sum for rented accommodation but he would be faced with renewing the lease or securing other space at the end of 15 years, in all probability at a higher rent. However, the additional space would not be available immediately: this may prove to be a significant factor in his deliberations.

Example
A enjoys a long lease of a building where he is responsible for all outgoings. He has recently replaced an outworn lift installation at a cost of £20 000 and anticipates a useful life of 15 years. Service charges are estimated at £750 per annum. His other costs of occupation include rent at £10 000 per annum, external maintenance and insurance estimated at £2350 per annum and internal redecoration every 5 years estimated to cost £2500. He wishes to know the annual equivalent of the various items of expenditure over the 40 years unexpired term of his lease. The building will be demolished when the lease expires (ignore any terminal compensation).

Solution

Annual outgoings	rent	£10 000	
	maintenance etc.	2 350	
	lift service	750	13 100
Periodic redecoration		£ 2 500[(i)]	

PV of £1 at 8% in

5 years	0.680 583 2		
10 years	0.463 193 5		
15 years	0.315 241 7		
20 years	0.214 548 2		
25 years	0.146 017 9		
30 years	0.099 377 3		
35 years	0.067 634 5	1.986 596 3	4966

Renewals of lift at a cost of £20 000   £19 250[ii]

PV of £1 at 8% in

15 years	0.315 241 7		
30 years	0.099 377 3	0.414 619	7981
			12 947

AE — interest at 8%	0.08		
Sinking fund			
40 years at 4%			
(tax 50%)	0.021 046 8	0.101 046 8	1308

Annual equivalent of rent and other obligations[iii] £14 408

Notes

(i)   No allowance is made for periodic redecoration in the fortieth year as the building is to be demolished.

(ii) The cost of renewal reflects the absence of the usual service charge in the years in which the lift is renewed.

(iii) The true cost of annual and period maintenance work and of insurance is likely to be less than the cost indicated as such expenses would normally be chargeable against the profits of a business.

FURTHER READING

Cartlidge, D. P. (1973) *Cost Planning and Building Economics*, Hutchinson Educational, London.

Clifton, R. H. (1974) *Principles of Planned Maintenance*, Edward Arnold, London.

Lee, R. (1976) *Building Maintenance Management*, Crosby Lockwood Staples, St Albans.

CHAPTER 11

Taxation

11.1 INTRODUCTION

Tax legislation has reached the point where most financial benefits, whether of an income or a capital nature are either subject to assessment or expressly exempt: they are not ignored. With the exception of income tax, the rest of the machinery has been developed since 1965 but in a piecemeal and unconnected fashion and subject to numerous subsequent additions, deletions and amendments. Not surprising, then, that the result is exceedingly difficult to comprehend, relate and integrate.

But the likelihood of a thorough-going review and consolidation of this area of the law is remote: instead the yearly Finance Act is used to tinker with the mechanism and spread the sources of the law ever wider.

Against this backcloth, it is one of the duties of the property manager to advise his client as to the most advantageous way in which to order his affairs. Where the problem is of sufficient importance, specialist advice will often be obtained but the property manager should be able to make an intelligent contribution to the deliberations.

The following sections are not intended to do more than highlight the main structure of each type of tax to enable the reader to recognize the more obvious warning signals.

11.2 REVENUE TAXES

Most income from property is subject to tax, mainly under Schedule A but in some cases under Schedule D. The income is regarded as unearned and currently subject to an investment income surcharge above a certain annual minimum sum. Where the income is received by a company it is subject to corporation tax. The incidence of the various taxes on income is outlined below.

11.2.1   Income tax

Income tax on receipts from property may be charged in a variety of ways

(a) Schedule A
(b) Schedule D
(c) Corporation tax

(a) *Schedule A*

(i) Unfurnished lettings

Assessments are on a current year basis, liability being calculated on the basis of the previous year's profit and adjusted when the correct figures are known. The gross rent may be simply in respect of use and enjoyment or may include sums in respect of outgoings such as repairs and insurance for which the owner is responsible. When during the currency of the lease the owner incurs expenditure on items such as maintenance, repair, services, rates, insurance, rent payable to a superior landlord and management, he may deduct these amounts from the rent receivable (regardless of whether it has been received) in computing the profit. Rent, or damages in lieu of rent, recovered through the courts is liable to tax.

There is an extra-statutory concession under which the cost of limited improvements may be deductible to the extent that they obviate the need for repairing the existing item.

Any insurance payment in respect of a sinking fund for the replacement of capital is disallowed, as is the expense of strategic management of an estate as opposed to the management of the individual properties comprised within that estate.

The cost of making good defects or dilapidations present on the acquisition of a property is regarded as capital expenditure and therefore not eligible as deductible expenditure for income tax purposes. It may well be relevant in computing a capital gain.

Where the property is let at a full rent any loss may be carried forward and set off against future rents from that property or in certain cases against rent from other property let at a full rent, but not against income assessable under any other schedule. 'Full rent' is defined to mean nothing more than a rent which is adequate, taking one year with another, to enable the lessor to discharge his obligations under the lease. For this purpose, any premium paid will be apportioned over the length of the lease.

Furnished lettings may be assessed under this schedule but are usually included under Schedule D.

(ii) Mineral royalties

Sums receivable by the owner of land in respect of mineral royalties are dealt with in a special way. Half the sum is treated as income and thus liable to income tax, the other half being treated as capital and liable to tax as a capital gain. Management expenses are allowed to the extent of one half of the total sum. Payment of royalties is made net of tax to the owner who may reclaim any overpayment after deduction of his liabilities for income tax and capital gains tax.

(iii) Rentcharges and other payments

Rentcharges and similar recurrent payments issuing from land are dealt with under Schedule A as are most of the other types of income from land with the specific exception of wayleaves, royalties, tolls, etc.

(iv) Premiums

Where a lease is granted for a term of 50 years or less and part of the consideration is paid to the landlord in the form of a premium or capital sum, there are special provisions for treatment of the amount received. The premium may be in the usual form of a capital sum or in some other form, as where the tenant is required to carry out work as a condition of the grant of the lease. In such a case, the landlord is regarded as having received a premium of an amount equal to the increase in the value of the reversion immediately on completion of the work, rather than the cost of carrying out the work. Except where the lessor is a trader in land (a term of art not easily defined but distinguishing broadly between someone who buys and sells as a business from another whose buying and selling is incidental to ownership) the premium will be treated partly as income assessable to income tax with the remainder as capital subject to capital gains tax. In calculating the length of the lease there will be taken into account the likelihood of an option to determine or to renew being exercised, assuming that all transactions are at arm's length.

There are rules for the calculation of that part of the premium subject to income tax. For each *complete* period of twelve months after the first twelve months, 2% of the total premium is deducted to arrive at the amount of the portion of the premium liable to income tax.

Example

Assume a lease granted for a term of fifteen years at a premium of £10 000.

Length of lease	15 years
Deduct first twelve months	1
Balance at 2% for each of	14 years = 28%
28% of £10 000 = £2800	

which is to be deducted from the premium leaving

£7200

This amount is added to the rent receivable in that year and the total is subject to income tax after making allowance for any deductible expenses. Where the premium is large, the landlord may find that the liability for income tax is greater than it would have been had no initial premium been charged but the amount spread over the term of the lease in the form of additional rent. In such a case, there is provision for 'top-slicing' relief.

The additional rent for this purpose is calculated by dividing the portion subject to income tax by the number of years granted by the lease or anticipated under it. To take the above example

$$\frac{\text{portion subject to income tax}}{\text{number of years}} \quad \frac{£7200}{15} = £480$$

when the tax payable under the alternative calculations may
be compared and relief claimed if appropriate. Where the
premium is payable to a person other than the landlord, the
recipient is assessable under Schedule D.

(b) *Schedule D*

Furnished lettings are normally dealt with under Schedule D
as are receipts from ancillary services such as provision of
caretaker or cleaning of the common areas. Where the taxpayer provides additional material services such as meals it is
likely that he will be treated as carrying on a trade and the
profit from the supply of services as earned income. Otherwise the income is dealt with as unearned income under
Case VI except that the taxpayer may elect within two years
to be assessed under Schedule A in respect of the property,
the payment for use of furniture remaining under Case VI: his
decision will be affected by the source of his other income
or losses. It is possible to offset profits under Case VI against
losses under Case VI but not against losses under Schedule A.

The tax may be assessed on a current year or a previous
year basis, the latter being more usual. In addition to deduction of expenses from the gross receipts, the taxpayer is able
to claim capital allowances in respect of the furniture. He
may claim either the full cost of replacements as and when
they take place or an annual percentage deduction from the
gross rents or the adjusted gross rents where the tenants meet
expenditure which would normally be the responsibility of
the landlord.

(c) *Corporation tax*

Corporation tax applies to limited and unlimited companies
and to certain associations. Rents are charged to corporation
tax in accordance with the rules applicable to Schedule A or
D. There are elaborate provisions relating to the status and
liability of companies and others subject to corporation tax,
the details of which are beyond this summary.

11.2.2   Rates

The rates levy is a particular form of revenue tax levied by the local rating authority and charged selectively, not according to income or ability to pay, but in respect of occupation of most, but not all, buildings. The levy is controlled only indirectly and then clumsily by the Government, even though the amount raised influences the support grant received from central government. The principal piece of legislation is the *General Rate Act 1967*. The basis of assessment is the annual value of each property, known as a hereditament, the occupier being responsible for payment except as noted later.

Dwelling-houses, private garages not exceeding 24 m^2 and private storage premises are assessed to gross value, the net annual value being calculated by deducting certain statutory allowances from the gross value. All other hereditaments are assessed directly to net annual value or rateable value.

Gross value is defined to mean the rent at which the hereditament might reasonably be expected to let from year to year if the tenant undertook to pay all usual tenant's rates and taxes and if the landlord undertook to bear the costs of the repairs and insurance and the other expenses, if any, necessary to maintain the hereditament in a state to command that rent.

The deductions from gross value to arrive at net annual or rateable value are set out in Table 11.1 Rates are chargeable on occupation which must be actual, beneficial, exclusive and not too transient. There are exemptions from rate liability, among them being property occupied by the Crown (though certain contributions are made in lieu of rates) land in public occupation and agricultural land and buildings used solely for agricultural purposes (subject to special bases applicable to farmhouses and agricultural workers' cottages, the effect of both of which is to confer an element of under assessment), places of worship, church halls and buildings in similar use, canals, railways and sewers (treatment works are rateable). Adjustments are made to exclude certain provision for the handicapped. Chattels are not rateable in general but certain chattels such as workmen's huts and kiosks have been held to be rateable where used in conjunction with land even though not fixed to the ground.

Table 11.1   Statutory deductions (*General Rate Act 1967* section 19(2))

Gross value	Deductions from gross value
Not exceeding £65	45% of GV
Between £66 and £128	£29 plus 30% of amount by which GV exceeds £65
Between £129 and £330	£48 plus $16\frac{2}{3}$% of amount by which GV exceeds £128, subject to a maximum of £80
Between £331 and £430	£80 plus 20% of amount by which GV excees £330
Exceeding £430	£100 plus $16\frac{2}{3}$% of amount by which GV exceeds £430

Plant and machinery are not rateable except for those types specified in *Land and Machinery Orders* made in 1960 and amended in 1974 and included in five classes which may be summarized as follows:

Class 1	A	Power plant
	B	Service plant
2		Passenger lifts
3		Railways and tramways
4		Plant in the nature of a building or structure
5		Pipelines

Where a charity is in occupation of premises used wholly or mainly for the purposes of the charity, it is entitled to claim relief as of right to the extent of one-half of the amount nominally payable. The rating authority may further reduce or remit in total, rates payable by a charity or similar body. Rebates are available to occupiers of residential accommodation whose income is below certain levels. The Act provided for the valuation list to be revised every five years. The last revision took place in 1973 and the *Local Government and Planning Act 1980* has dispensed with this requirement. The Secretary of State has power to make an order specifying when a new valuation list is to come into force.

The ratepayer or the rating authority may make a proposal

for alteration of the list as may the valuation officer. The figure proposed need not be stated: it is sufficient to indicate whether an increase or a decrease is sought. The proposer is required to state the grounds on which the alteration is proposed. It is sufficient to state that the present assessment is incorrect. Where a proposal is made by the ratepayer, it is usual to allege that the assessment is 'unfair, incorrect and excessive'.

The procedure is subject to time limits with a right of appeal to the local valuation court and from there to the Lands Tribunal with a further appeal to the Court of Appeal on a point of law. Any alteration takes effect from the beginning of the rate period during which the proposal is served unless the hereditament is new either because it is newly constructed or as a result of structural alterations. Then it takes effect from the date of completion of the new or altered building. Attempts to delay liability for payment of rates have led to various provisions. In the case of new buildings, the local authority may serve a completion notice specifying the time within which the completion or alterations may reasonably be expected to be completed, being not less than three months from the date of the notice. Subject to a right of appeal to the County Court the rate becomes payable on expiry of the notice.

In more buoyant times, commercial buildings sometimes remained unoccupied and unlet as part of a deliberate investment strategy. To counteract what was regarded as an undesirable use of the law, a surcharge was introduced which is penal in nature and sometimes unfair in operation.

Where a commercial building is left vacant for a period of six months or more the property may be liable to a charge (where the local authority has resolved to implement the surcharge provisions) from the first date when it became vacant: periods of use of six weeks or less are treated as non-use and ignored in considering liability to the surcharge which is registrable as a local land charge against the property. Similarly, where only part of the building is in use, occupation of less than four-fifths is treated as being non-use of the whole. The surcharge is based on the normal rates payable had the property been occupied. The amount payable is 100% in the first year increasing each year by 100% without limit. These penal provisions do not apply where it can be shown to the satisfaction of the rating authority that the owner has made proper efforts to let or sell the property according to criteria laid down in regulations. The authority has no discretion where it concludes that the owner has not satisfied the tests.

No surcharge is payable where the building is unfit for use and incapable of being rendered so at reasonable cost, where relevant works are being carried out to the extent that the building cannot reasonably be used, that it is proposed to carry out such works, where the owner is the personal representative or is bankrupt or in the case of a company, in voluntary or compulsory liquidation.

The Act defines a commercial building as any hereditament with a rateable value exceeding £2000 with the exception of

(a) A dwelling-house
(b) A lock-up garage or a motor garage constructed or adapted for use wholly in connection with a dwelling house for the parking of motor vehicles, in either case with a floor space not exceeding 240 square feet
(c) Private storage premises
(d) An industrial building or a building constructed or adapted as a factory and similar premises for use wholly or mainly for industrial purposes

A rating authority may resolve that the person entitled to possession is rated at one-half the normal rate where the hereditament is unoccupied for a continuous period of three months. Exemptions apply in respect of properties unoccupied in compliance with the law and for the first six months after completion in the case of a newly erected and unoccupied dwelling-house.

Finally, the rating authority may resolve that owners rather than occupiers shall be rateable in respect of certain premises with low rateable values. No hereditament may be included where the rateable value exceeds £200. The rating authority may fix a lower rateable value limit. An owner who lets property on a weekly or monthly basis may agree with the rating authority to pay the rates to them in which case he is entitled to an allowance of up to 10% depending on the circumstances:

(a) Where he merely collects rates on behalf of the rating authority 5%
(b) Where he agrees to be responsible for the payment of rates for any period for which the hereditament is occupied 7½%
(c) Where he agrees to be responsible for the payment of rates regardless of whether the hereditament is occupied or not 10%

The finance of local authority expenditure has long been a source of discussion and argument. Recent substantial increases in the rate burden have renewed pressure from hard pressed residential and business ratepayers for the introduction of a more equitable way of raising local taxes as pledged by the Conservative party prior to the 1979 election.

The House of Commons Environment Committee issued a Green Paper and as a result of the ensuing discussion and further deliberation has now produced a second report, the main conclusions of which are that rating must remain as the source of local authority funding and that capital values should replace rental values as the basis of assessment.

The Government has, predictably, rejected the idea of a local income tax on the basis that there is no evidence of support for such a move. An interesting notion which, if applied to national taxation, would have far-reaching ramifications.

11.2.3   Value added tax

Value added tax (VAT) was introduced in 1973 as a tax on the supply of goods and services.

The supply may be chargeable at the current rate of tax, be zero-rated or be exempt. Where a supply is taxable or zero-rated, the supplier may recover any input tax which he has paid even when, as in the case of zero-rated supplies, no output tax is charged (to the recipient or consumer). Less favourable is the exempt category because again no output tax is charged but in this case no input tax may be recovered. A person who supplies goods and services must be registered except where his turnover does not exceed a prescribed figure in which case he may register but is not compelled to do so. Where a builder sells or leases for a term exceeding twenty one years a building which he has constructed on land which he owns the transaction is zero-rated. Where the vendor is not a builder or where no building is erected the transaction is exempt regardless of the length of term granted. Goods and services supplied by a builder in the construction, reconstruction, alteration or demolition of any building are zero-rated though the fees of an architect, surveyor or other consultant are taxable.

Maintenance and repair work are liable to VAT as are services provided to part of a building occupied by a tenant and charged for separately. Where the payment is for up-keep of the building as a whole it may be exempt but if it is a service charge which can be treated in the same way as rent it may be zero-rated. Fees for management services are taxable as are sporting and similar rights.

Where fire damage has occurred, reinstatement of the original building is liable to VAT whereas a new building is zero-rated as described above. When advising on the level of insurance cover the property manager faces a dilemma which is discussed in the chapter on outgoings.

11.3 CAPITAL TAXES

As has been seen, an income tax liability may be incurred on part of a capital sum — a premium — received on granting a lease of property. But the principal taxes applied to transactions of a capital nature are not relevant to income profits or gains. Capital gains tax was introduced in 1965 to become the first attempt to attach tax to capital profits as they were made. Subsequently, an element of sophistication has been introduced by the provisions for capital transfer tax, while development land tax is the latest in a series of attempts to harness the fruits of development value for the community as a whole which, it is argued, created the value in the first place.

Development land tax is not only the most far reaching: it takes priority over other capital taxes and is therefore considered first.

11.3.1 Development land tax

The primary capital tax in relation to development land is development land tax (DLT) any profits not within its ambit being swept up by capital gains tax, capital transfer tax and possibly income tax.

For the purpose of DLT a disposal includes not only freehold and leasehold estates but also the right to take a lease conferred by an agreement for a lease, any right in or over land and any right affecting the use of or disposition of land or the right to obtain such an interest. Neither transfer of land on death nor a gift *inter vivos* is a disposal for development land tax. It is provided that a bare trustee or a lender shall not be treated as owning an interest in the land but charities and pension funds are liable. In addition to actual total and part disposals, the Act introduced the concept of 'deemed disposals'. The rules as to the effective date of a transaction for tax purposes together with the date on which payment becomes due, are summarized in Table 11.2. DLT is payable on the amount of the realized development value due to the taxpayer in the year ending 31 March. The value is calculated according to the detailed rules set out in the Act, the purpose of which is to isolate the development value on which the tax is charged: any other increases may be the subject of other capital taxes. Where there is a deemed disposal, it is assumed that the land is disposed of and immediately re-acquired at the start of any material development. The taxpayer is able to adopt the highest of three base values for deduction from the realized development value thus minimizing the resultant figure on which tax is calculated. The base values are

Base A The taxpayer's acquisition cost, expenditure on relevant improvements, any increase in the current use value during the period of ownership but not prior to 1965, and where the interest was acquired before 1 May 1977 a 'special addition' and a 'further addition' (the latter in respect of relevant improvements)

Base B 115% of the current use value at the time of disposal and any expenditure on relevant improvements

Table 11.2 When disposal takes place for DLT and CGT and when payment of tax becomes due

Event	Disposal
Conveyance transfer or lease not preceded by contract or option	When completed
Conveyance transfer or lease preceded by	
(i) Unconditional contract	When contract exchanged
(ii) Conditional contract	When condition satisfied and contract exchanged
(iii) Option	When option exercised
Deemed disposal on commencement of project of material development	
(i) Total	Immediately prior to commencement of project
(ii) Part, where capital sum received	
(a) Disposal before sum received	Immediately prior to disposal
(b) All other cases	When sum received
Compulsory purchase	
(i) Usual cases	The earlier event of agreement or determination of compensation and entry by the authority on the land
(ii) Where acquisition by vesting declaration	When vesting declaration takes effect

Payment of tax due:
Capital gains tax — payable in one sum at the end of three months following the end of the year of assessment in which the disposal took place or thirty days from the making of the assessment whichever is the later.

Development land tax — three months after the date of the event which gives rise to the liability or thirty days from the making of the assessment whichever is the later.

Base C   115% of the current use value at the time of disposal and 115% of any expenditure on improvements

There are further rules for calculations on part disposals, mainly concerned with the apportionment of the items used in calculating the base values between the interest disposed of and the interest retained.

216 *Property Management*

The 'special addition' is 15% of the acquisition cost for every year of ownership to a maximum of four years where the land was acquired before 13 September 1974 and 10% again to a maximum of four years for land acquired after 12 September 1974 and before 1 May 1977. The 'further addition' is calculated by taking that proportion of expenditure on relevant improvements represented by the fraction of the special addition to the acquisition cost.

The above description and the following example are intended simply to suggest the implications of the tax: the reader involved in calculations for the purpose of this tax will wish to refer to the *Development Land Tax Act 1976*, subsequent Finance Acts and specialist texts.

Example

A freehold cinema was purchased in 1973 for £200000 when its current use value (CUV) was £150000. £37000 was spent on improvements to make it suitable for use as a factory and warehouse without which the current use value at the date of disposal would have been £260000. The improvement of the surrounding area has enabled the owner to sell the property in 1981 for development of shops. The price obtained is £550000, the current use value at that time being £280000. The incidental costs of acquisition were £3500 and of disposal £25000. What is the realized development value?

Solution

Consideration for disposal		£550000
Less incidental costs of disposal		25000
Net proceeds		525000

Base A

Consideration for acquisition	£150000		
Incidental costs of acquisition	3500		
Cost of acquisition		153500	
Cost of improvements		37000	
Less: CUV at disposal	280000		
CUV at disposal without improvement	260000	20,000	

Expenditure on relevant improvements		17 000
CUV at disposal	280 000	
Less CUV at acquisition	150 000	
Increase in CUV		130 000
Special addition: 4 x 15% x 153 500		92 100
Further addition: $17\,000 \times \dfrac{92\,100}{153\,500}$		10 200
Base A		402 800

Base B

CUV at disposal	£280 000	
Add 15%	42 000	
		322 000
Expenditure on relevant improvements	17 000	
Base B		339 000

Base C

Cost of acquisition		153 500
Expenditure on improvements		37 000
		190 500
Add 15%		28 575
Base C		219 075

Deduct highest of three bases (Base A)	402 800
Realized development value (RDV)	£122 200

Under current provisions the first £50 000 of the RDV is exempt from DLT, the balance being charged at a rate of 60%.

11.3.2 Capital gains tax

In 1965 for the first time the Finance Act introduced a tax on the increase in capital value during the period of ownership. Any disposal or deemed disposal of land not being a trading disposal or an adventure in the nature of trade or of land which was acquired, held as stock or developed with the object of realizing a gain is liable to capital gains tax (CGT) on the chargeable gain. In his Budget Speech of March 1981, the Chancellor announced that relief will be given as from March 1982 in respect of inflation, measured by the retail price index.

The tax applies to individuals, partnerships and trustees and to companies where the rate of tax is adjusted to take account of corporation tax paid on part of their chargeable gain.

Allowances are made for costs on acquisition and disposal, expenditure on capital improvements and on establishing, preserving or defending the title. An adjustment is necessary where land was owned prior to 6 April 1965. There are exemptions in respect of small disposals, the principal private residence of the taxpayer and relief where business premises are sold and replaced by others and where a person retires and disposes of his business or an interest in that business. There are special provisions for agricultural land and gifts to charities or certain public bodies.

So called short leases are treated differently as 'wasting' assets (see below).

Losses may be set off against gains. Husbands' and wives' gains and losses are treated separately.

Both capital transfer tax (CTT) and development land tax (DLT) may be payable in addition to CGT. CGT is not payable on death.

The following example illustrates the calculations necessary where a property is sold giving rise to a capital gain.

Example
Calculate the capital gain on a suite of offices purchased for £25 000 in 1960 and sold in 1981 for £65 000. The value in 1965 was £35 000.

Calculations
Market value basis

Proceeds of sale in 1981	£65 000
Value in 1965	35 000
Chargeable gain	30 000

Time apportionment basis

Proceeds of sale in 1981		65 000
Cost of purchase in 1960		25 000
Profit		40 000

Ownership before 1965	5 years	
after 1965	16 years	
Total period of ownership	21 years	

Chargeable gain $\dfrac{16}{21}$ x £40 000 = £30 476

The taxpayer is entitled to elect for the market value basis of assessment. If he wishes to do so, he must make an election within two years of the end of the tax year in which the disposal took place. The election is binding. The time apportionment basis is not available for land with development value where the land was acquired for value before 6 April 1965, is being sold at a price including development value and material development has been carried out since 17 December 1973.

Example

The facts given in the example of calculations for DLT (page 216) are considered from the point of view of CGT.

Consideration for disposal		£550 000
Less allowable expenditure:		
Consideration for acquisition £150 000		
Incidental costs of acquisition 3 500	153 500	
Expenditure on improvements	37 000	
Incidental costs of disposal	25 000	
		215 500
Chargeable gain ignoring DLT liability		334 500
Less realized development value		122 200
Chargeable gain		£212 300

A lease granted for a term exceeding fifty years (a 'long' lease) is liable only to CGT. A lease granted for fifty years or less (a 'short' lease) is liable to income tax under Schedule A on part and CGT on the remainder except in certain cases, principally where the lessor is trading. On the assignment of a short lease the acquisition price is reduced by a statutory formula (Table 11.3) to take account of the wasting nature of the asset. Where enhancement of the lease is undertaken, the expenditure is treated in the same way as the premium but calculated from the date incurred. The calculations necessary are illustrated by the following example.

Examples

(a) A lease with 35 years unexpired was acquired at an initial cost (premium) of £6000. Fifteen years later the lease is assigned for £5000.
(b) Same facts as (a) except that £3000 was expended on enhancement when the lease had 30 years unexpired and the lease is assigned for £6500.

(a)   Sale price   £5000

Acquisition price   £6000

Less reduction in acquisition price

$$£6000 \times \frac{(35 \text{ years} - 15 \text{ years})*}{35 \text{ years}}$$

$$£6000 \times \frac{(91.981 - 61.617)}{91.981} \qquad 3301 \qquad 2699$$

Chargeable gain   £2301

(b)   Sale price   £6500

Acquisition price   £6000

Less reduction (above)   3301   2699

Enhancement
  expenditure   3000

$$\text{Less reduction} \quad 3000 \times \frac{(87.330 - 61.617)}{87.330}$$

                                  833   2117   £4816

Chargeable gain   £1684

* Statutory percentages (see Table 11.3)

Table 11.3 Table for use in calculations of tax payable on the assignment of a lease at a premium (*Finance Act 1965* Schedule 8, paragraph 1)

Years	Percentage
50 (or more)	100
49	99.657
48	99.289
47	98.902
46	98.490
45	98.059
44	97.595
43	97.107
42	96.593
41	96.041
40	95.457
39	94.842
38	94.189
37	93.497
36	92.761
35	91.981
34	91.156
33	90.280
32	89.354
31	88.371
30	87.330
29	86.226
28	85.053
27	83.816
26	82.496
25	81.000
24	79.622
23	78.055
22	76.399
21	74.635
20	72.770
19	70.791
18	68.697
17	66.470
16	64.116
15	61.617
14	58.971
13	56.167
12	53.191
11	50.038
10	46.695
9	43.154
8	39.399
7	35.414
6	31.195
5	26.722
4	21.983
3	16.599
2	11.629
1	5.983
0	0

There are further detailed rules relating to part disposals, including the grant of a sub-lease, for which reference should be made to a taxation text.

11.3.3   Capital transfer tax

Capital transfer tax (CTT) is payable, subject to certain exemptions, on any gift or gratuitous transfer which reduces the value of the transferor's estate during his lifetime. It is payable also on the deemed transfer on death. A sale at full value is not therefore liable to CTT as it does not reduce the value of the transferor's estate.

Two novel features of the tax are that the amount of tax payable is based on the reduction in the value of the transferor's estate and that the rate of tax is determined by the cumulative total of all transfers after 26 March 1974.

The larger the total, the higher the rate of tax payable. Where the transferor is responsible for payment of tax on the transfer of an asset, the value of that asset is grossed up to arrive at the true value of the transfer. There is a deemed transfer on death: any transfer then or within three years prior to death attracts a higher scale of rates.

There is relief for quick succession which recognizes that there would otherwise be an element of double taxation where CTT is payable on a lifetime transfer and on death of the transferor within four years.

11.4   STAMP DUTY

Conveyances, assignments and lettings are liable to stamp duties subject to certain exemptions.

Tables 11.4 and 11.5 set out the current rates.

11.5   MISCELLANEOUS MATTERS

A consideration of the effect of various taxes cannot be complete without some consideration of any benefits available by way of allowances or incentives. In particular, capital allowances, development area grants and Enterprise Zone incentives may need to be taken into account in assessing

Table 11.4   Stamp duty on conveyance or transfer on sale or premium for a lease

Consideration or premium		Rate of duty where certified*
exceeding	not exceeding	
25 000	30 000	½% of value of consideration
30 000	35 000	1% of value of consideration
35 000	40 000	1½% of value of consideration
40 000		2% of value of consideration

* An instrument which is 'certified' at a particular amount is one which contains a statement certifying that the transaction effected by the instrument does not form part of a larger transaction or series of transactions in respect of which the amount or value, or aggregate amount or value, of the consideration exceeds that amount.

An instrument which is not certified attracts duty at the rate of 2% on the total consideration.

a particular situation. Each of these possibilities is now considered very briefly.

11.5.1   Capital allowances

Where a taxpayer (who may be a landlord, a tenant or an owner-occupier) incurs capital-expenditure on the construction or repair of an industrial building he is eligible for certain allowances (an industrial building is essentially a building used for manufacture, storage of materials processed, to be processed or used in manufacture or in relation to the working of a mineral deposit).

The taxpayer may claim an initial allowance based on the original expenditure (after deduction of any grant) and writing down allowance each year until the whole of the expenditure is used up. When the interest is disposed of or the lease comes to an end, it may be necessary to claim a balancing allowance or meet a balancing charge.

The level of capital allowances is extended in some cases where the property is within an Enterprise Zone. A comparison of the allowances available is contained in Table 11.6.

Table 11.5 Stamp duty on a lease — based on annual rent

Rent not exceeding (£)	Term not exceeding 7 years or indefinite (£)	Term exceeding 7 years but not 35 years (£)	Term exceeding 35 years but not 100 years (£)	Term exceeding 100 years (£)
5	nil	0.10	0.60	1.20
10	nil	0.20	1.20	2.40
15	nil	0.30	1.80	3.60
20	nil	0.40	2.40	4.80
25	nil	0.50	3.00	6.00
50	nil	1.00	6.00	12.00
75	nil	1.50	9.00	18.00
100	nil	2.00	12.00	24.00
150	nil	3.00	18.00	36.00
200	nil	4.00	24.00	48.00
250	nil	5.00	30.00	60.00
300	nil	6.00	36.00	72.00
350	nil	7.00	42.00	84.00
400	nil	8.00	48.00	96.00
450	nil	9.00	54.00	108.00
exceeding 450	£0.50 per £50 or part thereof	£1.00	£6.00	£12.00

On review — *ad valorem*: 10p per £100 or part of £100.

Furnished lettings — A letting agreement for any definite term less than a year of any furnished dwelling house or apartment where the rent for the term exceeds £100 attracts a fixed duty of £1.

Table 11.6 Rates of capital allowance as percentage of original cost

Type of premises	Enterprise Zone		Elsewhere	
	Initial	Annual	Initial	Annual
Plant	100	25	100	25
Small workshops*	100	25	100	25
Industrial buildings	100	25	75	4
Hotels	100	25	20	4
Commercial buildings	100	25	—	—

* Defined as: Industrial buildings with gross internal floor area not exceeding 2500 square feet where expenditure incurred after 26 March 1980 and before 27 March 1983.

11.5.2 Development area grants

A wide range of grant assistance is available to entrepreneurs willing to develop or expand their businesses in development areas. The emphasis is on the creation of jobs rather than buildings and such assistance is likely therefore to attract the manufacturer rather than the developer.

11.5.3 Enterprise Zones

The creation of a number of Enterprise Zones, intended to assist industry and stimulate employment, was announced in the Budget speech in 1980 and formally brought into being by the *Local Government and Planning Act* of that year.

Initially, thirteen zones were designated throughout the United Kingdom: recently, local authorities have been invited to apply for an additional eleven units proposed by the Department of the Environment. The attraction of the zones is to both developer and occupier. In addition to simplified planning procedures and exclusion from compliance with the regulations of Industrial Training Boards, there are monetary advantages including exemption from development land tax and from local general rates together with 100% capital allowances for corporation and income tax purposes on commercial and industrial buildings. It is anticipated that there will be a strict limitation on sites available for retail use.

FURTHER READING

Joseph, C. (1980) *Development Land Tax*, Oyez Publishing, London.
Mellows, A. R. (1978) *Taxation of Land Transactions*, Butterworths, London.
Wheatcroft, G. S. A. (ed.) *The Hambro Tax Guide* (annual), Macdonald and Jane's, London.

CHAPTER 12

Computers in property management

12.1 INTRODUCTION

Professional men have been slow to recognize the contribution which the new electronic technology is capable of making to the running of an efficient organization.

The effort required to make the changeover, the risks of failure, the substantial costs involved and the existence of a good deal of unnecessary jargon in the industry have all played their part in delaying the investigation that will highlight the benefits likely to accrue from the installation of appropriate equipment.

The introduction of cheap microcomputers and associated equipment for use in schools, the popularity of home computers and the use of on-line equipment in many shops and showrooms should go some way at least towards breaking down the barriers against the use of the technology in the professions.

The ability to gather, record, organize, analyse, respond to and transmit information offers opportunities which cannot be ignored.

The speed and accuracy of interpretation is superior to anything likely to have been experienced previously. Calculations and financial analyses which would have been considered impracticable by manual methods become routine, simple and quick. Properly set-up, routine aspects of the business would be carried out at a very high level of efficiency.

12.2 PROPERTY MANAGEMENT

Property management records and accounting lend themselves to computerization.

The size of the practice will determine the capacity required of the equipment and, to some extent, its degree of sophistication. In considering the various systems available, the possibility of providing services for the agency function of the office and for the firm's office accounts should be investigated.

In any event, the property manager will be able to evince particularly convincing reasons for introducing the new technology. The typical management activity, at least in private practice, is highly fragmented: the client may be an individual owning a few modest properties or an institution with a sizeable and diverse portfolio. The interest may be freehold or leasehold, the term may be long or short, the tenant a substantial public company, an individual trader or a residential occupier. The tenant may be responsible for all outgoings or the landlord may have some liability: maintenance and the provision of services may be undertaken initially by the landlord and recovered from each tenant by means of an apportioned service charge. The manager may be called upon to provide a comprehensive facility or to give only a part of his full service.

The routine work in management is often tedious and drawn out when performed manually and ideal for processing with the aid of computer technology. Complicated work, such as the allocation and apportionment of service charges will be dealt with within at the most a few minutes of receiving the initial information.

12.3   THE EQUIPMENT

The computer is the central unit in the modern office. The first electronic computer was produced commercially in 1951 but was used only by a few of the major companies and in some limited areas of government: it was a large and hugely expensive piece of equipment requiring an air conditioned room with a significant electrical supply and producing a problem of heat dissipation.

The intervening period to the late 1970s saw successive reductions in size and cost and an increase in the capacity of the unit until eventually the advent of the silicon chip enabled the computer industry to offer a small portable 'micro' computer at a price within the reach of even the modest business. There has been a quickening of interest amongst businessmen which is likely to be maintained by further reductions in price and size, an increase in memory facilities, easier programming and the possible use of direct speech, all in the foreseeable future.

The typical microcomputer consists of a keyboard very similar to that of a typewriter, connected to a screen displaying the information as it is typed. The information is lost when the machine is disconnected from the power supply so there is a need for information storage facilities: a simple tape recorder may be used with ordinary cassette tapes but a disk is used where speed is essential, the time taken in searching for stored information being very much less. The other indispensable piece of equipment is the word processor, a sophisticated automatic electric typewriter which will print as instructed from the microcomputer at speeds up to 16 characters per second. It is a simple matter to print letters, memoranda or formal documents in a standard format or with any desired additions, omissions or amendments.

Further equipment is available. The optical character reader will scan documents and transfer a copy to storage for future use. Equipment has been developed which is capable of transmitting copy to a distant user via the telephone. Drawings, sketches and diagrams can be transferred as easily as typewritten information. Specially adapted television receiving sets give access to commercially based information banks with a wide range of constantly updated information. Records no longer current may be stored compactly on microfilm and consulted when necessary by use of a microreader.

Any detailed appreciation of the equipment would be inappropriate as it would be likely to be out of date before publication. Developments are taking place continuously while the volume of sales and rivalry between manufacturers combine to produce competitive pricing.

12.4   THE SOFTWARE

The microcomputer may be used by the operator typing his instructions (termed a 'program') and receiving the result either on the display screen or as a permanent record from the connected printer.

Where the same instructions are likely to be given repeatedly, it is much more efficient for the operator to store his instructions on tape or disk in which case he need only summon the appropriate program and supply the necessary data, a much quicker process.

Programs may be written by the operator but they employ one of a number of special languages and an operator is rarely a specialist in program writing and design.

A number of companies now offer property management packages, usually in conjunction with particular equipment. It is unlikely that such packages will cater fully for every requirement of the property manager. Some companies are prepared to undertake a limited amount of modification and rewriting of programs. The alternative of having the programs written especially for the particular organization is extremely expensive though possibly less so if a programmer can be persuaded that there may be a market for his work. But in order to justify the expense of a custom-built package and to achieve something superior to that already on the market, the manager must be prepared to devote much time and thought to exactly what he requires and to wait for it to be produced.

The property management programs fall into two groups, operating programs and management information programs. Each property manager will have his particular requirements but it may be helpful to list some of the programs which could be utilized in a typical practice.

12.4.1   The operating programs

(a) A ledger sheet for each client to which all rents received and expenditure incurred are transferred. The balance to the credit of the client could be obtained in a matter of seconds together with other details if required, for example any rents due and not received

(b) A demand to be sent to tenants showing the amount of rent due together with any amounts for insurance and service charges. The program should incorporate a 'follow-up' procedure for unpaid rents

(c) Preparation of a statement for each client, showing the balance due to him for the accounting period

(d) A program for the allocation of service charges on the basis laid down for contributing tenants

(e) A commission account, enabling the property manager to determine the commissions due to him and to arrange for their transfer

(f) Programs may be written for any other operation necessary

12.4.2 The management information programs

With efficient programming, the manager should be able to increase his efficiency. The programs will act as a perfect memory, leaving him to take the necessary action. Useful programs would include

(a) A 'serious arrears' list enabling him to review outstanding rents at regular intervals and to take any of a number of actions including reporting to the owner, instructing the owner's solicitor or serving a notice to quit. In each case, the program could be written so as to produce the letter or notice

(b) A 'rent review' list. At a predetermined time before a review was due, the manager would receive a reminder enabling him to initiate the procedure required by the lease. The list would be produced at regular intervals and the property would continue to be listed until the review had been disposed of. There would be a similar program for tenancies coming to an end

(c) Insurance revaluations. The program would include details of floor areas, construction, age and other items relevant to the cost of replacement and the addition of information on current costs obtained from tenders or one of the cost indices available would enable an up-to-date figure to be calculated

(d) Asset valuations. Asset valuation work could be reduced by the recording of all permanent information to which the valuer would make any necessary alterations, add appropriate unit values and obtain figures to act as the basis of his valuation

(e) Terrier information. Extracts from the lease could be

stored for retrieval when required. For example, the manager could refer to any provisions relating to repair liabilities to establish responsibility for the necessary work

(f) Maintenance programs. Leases often specify when a tenant should carry out certain work: where the landlord is responsible for some aspects of maintenance it is desirable that it should be undertaken on a planned basis: in either case a program may act as a diary to remind the manager that he should be checking tenant's work or initiating procedures

(g) Projection programs. The manager may wish to estimate rental growth on behalf of his client or management fee income in relation to the future progress of his firm. In either case, the storage of readily accessible data on the computer facilitates such estimates

12.5   OTHER CONSIDERATIONS

The decision to use the new technology will raise a number of questions that need to be resolved, some of which will be touched on here.

12.5.1   Capacity

Should the hardware be capable of carrying out only the task for which it is required or should it anticipate further demands? The practice might decide to computerize other aspects of the firm's work or it may obtain further substantial management work beyond the capacity of the existing equipment. These present particularly difficult questions but it is likely that most firms will enter the area cautiously and without undue expenditure on contingencies not connected with the operation in hand. A relatively inexpensive system will soon demonstrate the possibilities of the technology and, in most cases, make the user keen to extend his system.

12.5.2   Security

The question of security of information is one that concerns many firms. It is natural that the prospect of unauthorized individuals obtaining access to confidential details raises fears. But there is no reason why the various programs should not contain restrictions on access: the more sophisticated systems are capable of recording who has used the stored information and which parts of the store have been consulted. Protection against loss by fire or other causes can be greatly superior to any system maintained by manual or mechanical means. Current information may be saved daily if required by making duplicate disks and placing them in a bank or elsewhere.

12.5.3 Stationery

It is likely to be advantageous to have at least some parts of the firm's stationery such as rent demands, reminders, orders and statements in the form of continuous perforated rolls designed for use in the printer attached to the computer. Where a word processor is included as part of the equipment used, the manager will no doubt wish to produce standard letters, agreement forms and similar items faster than otherwise and without any need to check the typing for errors.

12.5.4 Staff implications

The mix of staff abilities required is likely to change as a result of introducing the computer. A reduction in the amount of original typing and in making tedious entries in the accounts should result in fewer staff being required for those tasks. Whether the overall staff requirement reduces will depend upon the particular operation and whether more business is attracted by the increased efficiency. It is unlikely that the decision to introduce computer technology will be based wholly or mainly on the ensuing savings in staff.

12.5.5 Accommodation

At one time, it was necessary to have special air conditioned rooms in which to house the equipment, but this is not essential with microcomputers. Where there are two or more units connected to a central terminal it will be necessary to provide cableways between the main machine and its satellites.

12.5.6   Training

Careful enquiries should be made as to the amount of training available for operators initially and on staff changes. At least part of the training should be undertaken on the particular system to be used. It is usual to operate the old and new systems alongside one another for a period long enough to ensure that the new system is fully understood and being operated correctly.

12.6   CONCLUSION

We are witnessing a revolution in office technology. A minority of firms is taking part in it. The firms so far uncommitted fall into two groups: those which are anxious to keep up to date but have understandable reservations about the type of system to install and those which see no reason to change their present methods. The time is fast approaching when the normal means of communication between manager and client will be by computer (linked by telephone or land line) and it is doubtful whether the latter group would survive for long in those conditions. For the rest, the new technology offers the opportunity of providing a service efficient beyond any possible expectations of a few years ago: Elysium indeed.

FURTHER READING

Cecil, P. B. (1980) *Word Processing in the Modern Office*, Benjamin/Cummins.

O'Brien, J. A. (1979) *Computers in Business Management*, Irwin Dorsey, New York.

Scott, P. E. (1975) *Programming in BASIC*, English Universities Press, Sevenoaks.

Turner, M. J. L. (1980) *Buying a Business Computer*, Whitney on Wye.

Appendix

Form numbers 1 and 8 of the *Landlord and Tenant Act 1954* are reproduced here with the permission of the Controller of Her Majesty's Stationery Office.

SCHEDULE 2

Form Number 1

LANDLORD'S NOTICE TO TERMINATE BUSINESS
TENANCY*

(LANDLORD AND TENANT ACT 1954, SECTION 25)

To: *(name of tenant)*

of   *(address of tenant)*

IMPORTANT—THIS NOTICE IS INTENDED TO BRING YOUR TENANCY TO AN END. IF YOU WANT TO CONTINUE TO OCCUPY YOUR PROPERTY YOU MUST ACT QUICKLY. READ THE NOTICE AND ALL THE NOTES CAREFULLY. IF YOU ARE IN ANY DOUBT ABOUT THE ACTION YOU SHOULD TAKE, GET ADVICE IMMEDIATELY e.g. FROM A SOLICITOR OR SURVEYOR OR A CITIZENS ADVICE BUREAU.

1. This notice is given under section 25 of the Landlord and Tenant Act 1954.

---

*This form must *not* be used if—

(a) no previous notice terminating the tenancy has been given under section 25 of the Act, and

(b) the tenancy is the tenancy of a house (as defined for the purposes of Part 1 of the Leasehold Reform Act 1967), and

(c) the tenancy is a long tenancy at a low rent (within the meaning of that Act of 1967), and

(d) the tenant is not a company or other artificial person.

If the above apply, use form number 13 instead of this form.

2. It relates to ....
(description of property)
of which you are the tenant.

See notes 1
and 8.

3. I/we give you notice terminating your tenancy on ....

See notes 2
and 3.

4. If you are not willing to give up possession of the property comprised in the tenancy on the date stated in paragraph 3, you must notify me/us in writing within two months after the giving of this notice.

*The land-
lord must
cross out one
version of
paragraph 5.
If the second
version is
used the
paragraph
letter(s) must
be filled in.

5.* If you apply to the court under Part II of the Landlord and Tenant Act 1954 for the grant of a new tenancy, I/we will not oppose your application.

OR

See notes 4
and 5.

5.* If you apply to the court under Part II of the Landlord and Tenant Act 1954 for the grant of a new tenancy, I/we will oppose it on the grounds mentioned in paragraph(s) .... of section 30(1) of the Act.

†Cross out
words in
square
brackets
if they do
not apply.

6. All correspondence about this notice should be sent to †[the landlord] [the landlord's agent] at the address given below.

Date ....

Signature of †[landlord] [landlord's agent]

....

Name of landlord ....

Address of landlord ....

....

....

†[Address of agent ....

....

....]

NOTES

Termination of tenancy

1. This notice is intended to bring your tenancy to an end. You can apply to the court for a new tenancy under the Landlord and Tenant Act 1954 by following the procedure outlined in notes 2 and 3 below. If you do your tenancy will continue after the date shown in paragraph 3 of this notice while your claim is being considered. The landlord can ask the court to fix the rent which you will have to pay while the tenancy continues. The terms of any *new* tenancy not agreed between you and the landlord will be settled by the court.

Claiming a new tenancy

2. If you want to apply to the court for a new tenancy you must:—

(1) notify the landlord in writing not later than 2 months after the giving of this notice that you are not willing to give up possession of the property;

AND

(2) apply to the court, not earlier than 2 months nor later than 4 months after the giving of this notice, for a new tenancy. You should apply to the County Court unless the rateable value of the business part of your premises is above the current County Court limit. In that case you should apply to the High Court.

3. The time limits in note 2 run from the giving of the notice. The date of the giving of the notice may not be the date written on the notice or the date on which you actually saw it. It may, for instance, be the date on which the notice was delivered through the post to your last address known to the person giving the notice. If there has been any delay in your seeing this notice you may need to act very quickly. If you are in any doubt get advice immediately.

WARNING TO TENANT
IF YOU DO NOT KEEP TO THE TIME LIMITS IN NOTE 2, YOU WILL *LOSE* YOUR RIGHT TO APPLY TO THE COURT FOR A NEW TENANCY.

Landlord's opposition to claim for a new tenancy

4. If you apply to the court for a new tenancy, the landlord can only oppose your application on one or more of the grounds set out in section 30(1) of the 1954 Act. These grounds are set out below. The paragraph letters are those given in the Act. The landlord can only use a ground if its paragraph letter is shown in paragraph 5 of the notice.

Grounds

(a) where under the current tenancy the tenant has any obligations as respects the repair and maintenance of the holding, that the tenant ought not to be granted a new tenancy in view of the state of repair of the holding, being a state resulting from the tenant's failure to comply with the said obligations;

(b) that the tenant ought not to be granted a new tenancy in view of his persistent delay in paying rent which has become due;

(c) that the tenant ought not to be granted a new tenancy in view of other substantial breaches by him of his obligations under the current tenancy, or for any other reason connected with the tenant's use or management of the holding;

(d) that the landlord has offered and is willing to provide or secure the provision of alternative accommodation for the tenant, that the terms on which the alternative accommodation is available are reasonable having regard to the terms of the current tenancy and to all other relevant circumstances, and that the accommodation and the time at which it will be available are suitable for the tenant's requirements (including the requirement to preserve goodwill) having regard to the nature and class of his business and to the situation and extent of, and facilities afforded by, the holding;

(e) where the current tenancy was created by the sub-letting of part only of the property comprised in a superior tenancy and the landlord is the owner of an interest in reversion expectant on the termination of that superior tenancy, that the aggregate of the rents reasonably obtainable on separate lettings of the holding and the remainder of that property would be substantially less than the rent reasonably obtainable on a letting of that property as a whole, that on the termination of the current tenancy the landlord requires possession of the holding for the purposes of letting or otherwise disposing of the said property as a whole, and that in view thereof the tenant ought not to be granted a new tenancy;

(f) that on the termination of the current tenancy the landlord intends to demolish or reconstruct the premises comprised in the holding or a substantial part of those premises or to carry out substantial work of construction on the holding or part thereof and that he could not reasonably do so without obtaining possession of the holding;

(If the landlord uses this ground, the court can sometimes still grant a new tenancy if certain conditions set out in section 31A of the Act can be met.)

(g) that on the termination of the current tenancy the landlord intends to occupy the holding for the purposes, or partly for the purposes, of a business to be carried on by him therein, or as his residence.

(The landlord must normally have been the landlord for at least
five years to use this ground.)

Compensation

5. If you cannot get a new tenancy solely because grounds *(e)*, *(f)* or
(g) apply, you are entitled to compensation under the 1954 Act. If your
landlord has opposed your application on any of the other grounds as
well as *(e)*, *(f)* or *(g)* you can only get compensation if the Court's refusal
to grant a new tenancy is based solely on grounds *(e)*, *(f)* or *(g)*. In other
words you cannot get compensation under the 1954 Act if the Court has
refused your tenancy on *other* grounds even if *(e)*, *(f)* or *(g)* also apply.

6. If your landlord is an authority possessing compulsory purchase
powers (such as a local authority) you may be entitled to a disturbance
payment under Part III of the Land Compensation Act 1973.

Negotiating a new tenancy

7. Most leases are renewed by negotiation. If you do try to agree a
new tenancy with your landlord, remember—

(1) that your present tenancy will not be extended after the date in
paragraph 3 of this notice unless you *both*

(a) give written notice that you will not vacate (note 2(1) above); *and*

(b) apply to the court for a new tenancy (note 2(2) above);

(2) that you will lose your right to apply to the court if you do not
keep to the time limits in note 2.

Validity of this notice

8. The landlord who has given this notice may not be the landlord to
whom you pay your rent. "Business" is given a wide meaning in the
1954 Act and is used in the same sense in this notice. The 1954 Act also
has rules about the date which the landlord can put in paragraph 3. This
depends on the terms of your tenancy. If you have any doubts about
whether this notice is valid, get immediate advice.

Explanatory booklet

9. The Department of the Environment booklet "Business Tenancies" explains the provisions of Part II of the 1954 Act in more detail
than these notes. It is available from Her Majesty's Stationery Office or
through booksellers.

Form Number 8

TENANT'S REQUEST FOR NEW TENANCY OF BUSINESS PREMISES

(LANDLORD AND TENANT ACT 1954, SECTION 26)

To: *(name of landlord)*

of   *(address of landlord)*

> IMPORTANT—THIS IS A REQUEST FOR A NEW TENANCY OF YOUR PROPERTY OR PART OF IT. IF YOU WANT TO OPPOSE THIS REQUEST YOU MUST ACT QUICKLY. READ THE REQUEST AND ALL THE NOTES CAREFULLY. IF YOU ARE IN ANY DOUBT ABOUT THE ACTION YOU SHOULD TAKE, GET ADVICE IMMEDIATELY e.g. FROM A SOLICITOR OR SURVEYOR OR A CITIZENS ADVICE BUREAU.

1. This request is made under section 26 of the Landlord and Tenant Act 1954.

2. You are the landlord of ....
(description of property)

3. I/we request you to grant a new tenancy beginning on ....

4. I/we propose that:

(a) the property comprised in the new tenancy should be ....

....

(b) the rent payable under the new tenancy should be ....

....

(c) the other terms of the new tenancy should be ....

....

†Cross out words in square brackets if they do not apply.

5. All correspondence about this request should be sent to †[the tenant] [the tenant's agent] at the address given below.

Date ....

Signature of †[tenant] [tenant's agent]

....

Name of tenant ....

Address of tenant ....

....

....

†[Address of agent ....

....

....]

NOTES

Request for a new tenancy

1. This request by your tenant for a new tenancy brings his current tenancy to an end on the day before the date mentioned in paragraph 3 above. He can apply to the court under the Landlord and Tenant Act 1954 for a new tenancy. If he does, his current tenancy will continue after the date mentioned in paragraph 3 of this request while his application is being considered by the court. You can ask the court to fix the rent which your tenant will have to pay whilst his tenancy continues. The terms of any *new* tenancy not agreed between you and your tenant will be settled by the court.

Opposing a request for a new tenancy

2. If you do not want to grant a new tenancy, you *must* within two months of the making of this request, give your tenant notice saying that you will oppose any application he makes to the court for a new tenancy. You do not need a special form to do this, but you must state on which of the grounds set out in the 1954 Act you will oppose the application—see note 4.

3. The time limit in note 2 runs from the making of this request. The date of the making of the request may not be the date written on the request or the date on which you actually saw it. It may, for instance, be the date on which the request was delivered through the post to your last address known to the person giving the request. If there has been any delay in your seeing this request you may need to act very quickly. If you are in any doubt get advice immediately.

> WARNING TO LANDLORD
> IF YOU DO NOT KEEP TO THE TIME LIMIT IN NOTE 2, YOU WILL *LOSE* YOUR RIGHT TO OPPOSE YOUR TENANT'S APPLICATION TO THE COURT FOR A NEW TENANCY IF HE MAKES ONE.

Grounds for opposing an application

4. If your tenant applies to the court for a new tenancy, you can only oppose the application on one or more of the grounds set out in section 30(1) of the 1954 Act. These grounds are set out below. The paragraph letters are those given in the Act.

Grounds

(a) where under the current tenancy the tenant has any obligations as respects the repair and maintenance of the holding, that the tenant ought not to be granted a new tenancy in view of the state of repair of the holding, being a state resulting from the tenant's failure to comply with the said obligations;

(b) that the tenant ought not to be granted a new tenancy in view of his persistent delay in paying rent which has become due;

(c) that the tenant ought not to be granted a new tenancy in view of other substantial breaches by him of his obligations under the current tenancy, or for any other reason connected with the tenant's use or management of the holding;

(d) that you have offered and are willing to provide or secure the provision of alternative accommodation for the tenant, that the terms on which the alternative accommodation is available are reasonable having regard to the terms of the current tenancy and to all other relevant circumstances, and that the accommodation and the time at which it will be available are suitable for the tenant's requirements (including the requirement to preserve goodwill) having regard to the nature and class of his business and to the situation and extent of, and facilities afforded by, the holding;

(e) where the current tenancy was created by the sub-letting of part only of the property comprised in a superior tenancy and you are the owner of an interest in reversion expectant on the termination of that superior tenancy, that the aggregate of the rents reasonably obtainable on separate lettings of the holding and the remainder of that property would be substantially less than the rent reasonably obtainable on a letting of that property as a whole, that on the termination of the current tenancy you require possession of the holding for the purpose of letting or otherwise disposing of the said property as a whole, and that in view thereof the tenant ought not to be granted a new tenancy;

(f) that on the termination of the current tenancy you intend to demolish or reconstruct the premises comprised in the holding or a substantial part of those premises or to carry out substantial work of construction on the holding or part thereof and that you could not reasonably do so without obtaining possession of the holding;

(If you use this ground, the court can sometimes still grant a new tenancy if certain conditions set out in section 31A of the Act can be met.)

(g) that on the termination of the current tenancy you intend to occupy the holding for the purposes, or partly for the purposes, of a business to be carried on by you therein, or as your residence.

(You must normally have been the landlord for at least five years to use this ground.)

You can only use one or more of the above grounds if you have stated them in the notice referred to in note 2 above.

Compensation

5. If your tenant cannot get a new tenancy solely because grounds *(e)*, *(f)* or *(g)* apply, he is entitled to compensation from you under the 1954 Act. If you have opposed his application on any of the other grounds as well as *(e)*, *(f)* or *(g)* he can only get compensation if the court's refusal to grant a new tenancy is based solely on grounds *(e)*, *(f)* or *(g)*. In other words he cannot get compensation under the 1954 Act if the court has refused his tenancy on *other* grounds even if *(e)*, *(f)* or *(g)* also apply.

6. If you are an authority possessing compulsory purchase powers (such as a local authority) you will be aware that your tenant may be entitled to a disturbance payment under Part III of the Land Compensation Act 1973.

Negotiating a new tenancy

7. Most leases are renewed by negotiation. If you do try to agree a new tenancy with your tenant—

(1) YOU should remember that you will not be able to oppose an application to the court for a new tenancy unless you give the notice mentioned in note 2 above within the time limit in that note;

(2) YOUR TENANT should remember that he will lose his right to apply to the court for a new tenancy unless he makes the application not less than two nor more than four months after the making of this request.

Validity of this notice

8. The landlord to whom this request is made may not be the landlord to whom the tenant pays the rent. "Business" is given a wide meaning in the 1954 Act and is used in the same sense in this request. The 1954 Act also has rules about the date which the tenant can put in paragraph 3. This depends on the terms of the tenancy. If you have any doubts about whether this request is valid, get immediate advice.

Explanatory booklet

9. The Department of the Environment booklet "Business Tenancies" explains the provisions of Part II of the 1954 Act in more detail than these notes. It is available from Her Majesty's Stationery Office or through booksellers.

Index